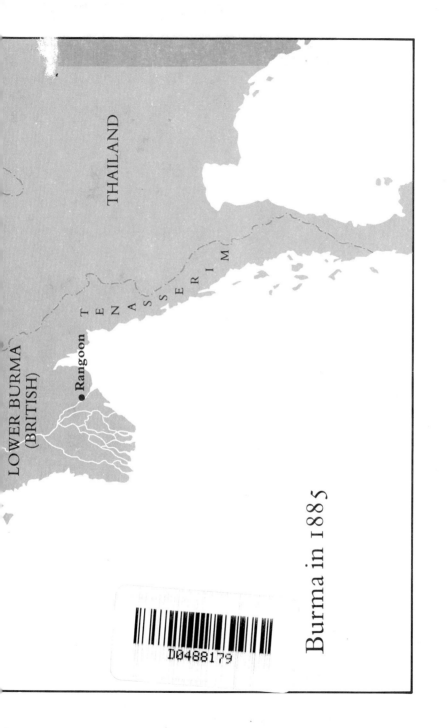

THAILAND

LOWER BURMA
(BRITISH)

● **Rangoon**

T
E
N
A
S
S
E
R
I
M

Burma in 1885

IMAGES OF ASIA

Burmese Dance and Theatre

Titles in the series

Burmese Dance and Theatre

NOEL F. SINGER

KUALA LUMPUR
OXFORD UNIVERSITY PRESS
OXFORD SINGAPORE NEW YORK
1995

Press

rk

ɔk Bombay

Salaam Delhi

ıbul Karachi

Mexico City

Nairobi Paris Shah Alam Singapore
Taipei Tokyo Toronto

and associated companies in
Berlin Ibadan

Oxford is a trade mark of Oxford University Press

Published in the United States
by Oxford University Press, New York

© Oxford University Press 1995
First published 1995

British Library Cataloguing in Publication Data
Data available
Library of Congress Cataloging-in-Publication Data
Singer, Noel F. (Noel Francis), 1937-
Burmese dance and theatre/Noel F. Singer.
p. cm.—(Images of Asia)
Includes bibliographical references (p.) and index.
ISBN 967 65 3086 7:
1. Dance—Burma—History.   2. Theater—Burma—History.   I. Title.
II. Series.
GV1703.B95S46   1995
793.3' 19591—dc20
94–41033
CIP

Typeset by Indah Photosetting Centre Sdn. Bhd., Malaysia
Printed by KHL Printing Co. Pte. Ltd., Singapore
Published by the South-East Asian Publishing Unit,
a division of Penerbit Fajar Bakti Sdn. Bhd.,
under licence from Oxford University Press,
4 Jalan U1/15, Seksyen U1, 40000 Shah Alam,
Selangor Darul Ehsan, Malaysia

*To all who have kept alive the
traditional performing arts of the country*

Preface and Acknowledgements

THE performing arts of the country of my birth have always held a deep fascination for me. In my youth, I not only collected relevant literature, but attended numerous theatrical performances and learnt some of the difficult dance movements.

A Burmese play may be incapable of creating the electrifying atmosphere of the Kabuki and No theatres of Japan. Its dances may lack the formality of the *mudra* (gestures) which dominate dance forms of India. On the other hand, however, Burmese dance movements are bright and spontaneous, and their sparkling exuberance personifies the charming and benign side of the nation's character.

In the Burma of the 1950s and early 1960s that I knew, I was also intrigued by the dialogue of the old plays and by *ngo-chin* (weeping songs), which are composed in High Burmese and either recited or sung. As the use of these songs is now considered unlucky and inappropriate in an independent country, some of the published versions will probably face extinction, while the survivors will be consigned to some dusty shelf in a library. It is to be hoped that far-sightedness prevails among those who control the future of Burma, and that the traditional performing arts of the country will never be allowed to die.

Several people have helped me in the preparation of this book. I should like to thank the Victoria and Albert Museum for permission to reproduce a rare painting of a propitiation ceremony at Taungbyon, near Mandalay. I also wish to acknowledge the invaluable help I have always received from that doyenne of Burmese culture, Sylvia Fraser-Lu, particularly for her generosity with much-needed illustrations.

Thanks also go to Patricia Herbert of the British Library, Shwebo Mi Mi Gyi in Mandalay, and Paul Strachan of Kiscadale Publications for sharing his experience of a recent theatrical performance. I am eternally grateful to Terence Blackburn for reading the manuscript and advising on changes for improvement. I also wish to acknowledge the splendid support and advice I have always received from the editorial staff at Oxford University Press.

Finally, my *ka-daw-pwe* (offerings) of gratitude and special thanks must go to the multitude of Burmese authors from whose published works I have plundered—shamelessly.

Bedfordshire   NOEL F. SINGER
1994   (NAY MYO)

Contents

Introduction

As the capitals of both the Pyu and the Mon, the two early civilized races in Burma, were close to the commercial sea lanes, they were in contact with the cultures of India and South-East Asia. Missions from abroad were sometimes accompanied by entertainers who left an impression on their hosts. Foreign and indigenous styles mingled, and were adopted, or adapted to local tastes.

Although court rituals and ceremonies were based on Buddhist and Hindu beliefs, there was religious freedom. Commoners believed in animistic cults, together with an elementary form of Buddhism. Propitiation ceremonies to the spirits, with music, song, and dance evolved, and these were later to influence strolling players.

In 1057, the Mon kingdom of Thaton was sacked by the Burmese, and its clergy and craftsmen were induced to assist in transforming their conqueror's capital, Pagan. Thousands of temples were built, and the city became renowned as a Buddhist haven until 1287 when an invasion by the Mongols ended the ruling dynasty. Power shifted from the Burmese to Shan warlords, who assumed sovereignty, and the petty kingdoms which emerged fought each other for the next two and a half centuries.

It was Burmese tradition to take skilled craftsmen from a conquered state to the capital, thereby improving the quality of the indigenous arts. Between wars there were bursts of creative activity, in which the secular and the religious sectors benefited. The main influence in music, dance, and drama of the court, and of the common people, came from Thailand. This was particularly true during the sixteenth and eighteenth centuries. Under the kings of the Konbaung Dynasty (1752–1885), the Burmese clashed with the British in India, resulting in the wars of 1824 and 1852. Hostilities between the Burmese and the British resumed in 1885, and with the annexation of Upper Burma, the whole country became part of the British Empire.

The former court performers mingled with the strolling players, and in some partnerships raised the standard of the theatre However, this was a period of change, and some of the old traditions were replaced and new dance items introduced. Live theatrical performances which previously could only be presented at ground level, adopted the Western-style stage.

In the early 1940s, Burma was occupied by the Japanese Army, but was liberated in 1945. The country gained its independence from the British in 1948, only to plunge into civil war between various political factions.

Stability of sorts returned in the early 1950s, and public performances resumed. State Schools for the Fine Arts were opened to teach a new generation of performers. During the last thirty years, while shows by professionals have slowly deteriorated, amateur groups have preserved and maintained traditional dance forms. However, plans for the encouragement and preservation of the performing arts are now under way. The present military government recently sponsored contests in singing, dancing, music, and drama.

1

Events in the World of
the Performing Arts until 1885

IN AD 800, the maharaja of the Pyu city of Sri Kshetra was ordered by his overlord, I-mou-hsun (r. 778–808), ruler of Nanchao (Yunnan), to send a cultural troupe to accompany the ruler's entertainers to the T'ang court at Ch'ang-an. A mission duly left the capital, taking with it a troupe of Pyu dancers and Mon musicians. The hazardous journey, which began in June 801, was to last 214 days.

It is recorded in the *Hsin-t'ang-shu* [The New T'ang History] that in February 802, thirty-five Piao (Pyu) entertainers appeared with an embassy from Nanchao. Among the thirty-two musical instruments they brought were dragon-headed lutes, mouth organs with sixteen pipes, and drums covered in snakeskin. It noted that the dancers (Colour Plate 1) were dressed in silk-cotton and gauze-silks, and adorned themselves with gold ornaments, jewelled caps, and diadems. According to the account, a Pyu master of ceremonies explained the meaning of each item before it commenced. Twelve songs on Buddhist themes were sung, and the dancers, among whom were tattooed men, performed in groups, which varied in size from two to ten performers. They nodded their 'flowery crowns' and whirled with 'the motion of dragon or snake' and, at the end of the show, lined up with I-mou-hsun's dancers to form Chinese characters which read 'Nanchao sends holy music'.

Emperor Dezong (r. 779–805) was so impressed that he bestowed minor titles on the leaders of the troupe of 'barbarians', and offered friendship. But the T'ang court was far removed from the city of Sri Kshetra, and when in 832 Nanchao turned on the Pyu and ravaged their kingdom, the Chinese could not come to its aid. The Pyu lost their dominance, and were eventually absorbed by the more militant Burmese.

The *Man-shu-chiao-chu* [Book of the Southern Barbarians] (860–73) noted that the citizens of the Mon city of Mi-ch'en were fond of wine, and liked to dance to the sound of drums

1

which hung at each end of their long houses. However, they too were attacked by Nanchao in 835. While the Pyu never recovered, the Mon regrouped at Thaton, until invaded by the Burmese King Aniruddha (r. 1044–77) in 1057. He relocated the inhabitants of the city to his capital Pagan, and took into service those with specialist skills, including the entertainers of the Mon king. In time, some of the Burmese, Pyu, and Mon dance and music traditions merged and evolved into a single style.

From the time of Aniruddha, there were specialist establishments called Gamawati Pwe-kyaung for training people in the performing arts. These centres were run by a Buddhist sect known as the Ari. Although religious instruction was also given, the emphasis was on a variety of secular subjects, including singing, dancing, and music (U Tin, 1932–3).

At Pagan, interest in the performing arts was already evident by the eleventh century, with dancers and musicians being featured in works of art. In particular, the carvings on the doors of Aniruddha's Shwezigon Pagoda depict entertainers in a variety of poses and dancing to the music of drums and trumpets. The movements are remarkably Indian, with the legs held open and bent at the knees (a posture avoided by modern Burmese female dancers).

In the Shwesandaw Inscription of 1093, Htihlaing Min (r. 1084–1112) noted that his subjects came to court on homage days singing and dancing 'in the fashion of every country district, town, every village, and all the jungle folk'. They appeared dressed 'in the semblance of all manner of creatures, of all sorts of demons, and gods'. This would suggest that the people of the period were capable of designing costumes and masks. Indeed, a plaque in the Ananda Temple, built by the king in 1091, depicts a dancing girl wearing a dragon head-dress.

Visual evidence of musical instruments indicates that the double-headed drum was popular. The resonating surfaces were made of deerskin, with thongs to keep them taut. At court, the right-voluted conch shell was blown on important occasions and during solo dances. Other wind instruments were the *kha-yar* (several kinds of trumpet) and reed pipes. Drawings of the boat-shaped harp show that it had seven strings. There were also cymbals, flutes, gongs,

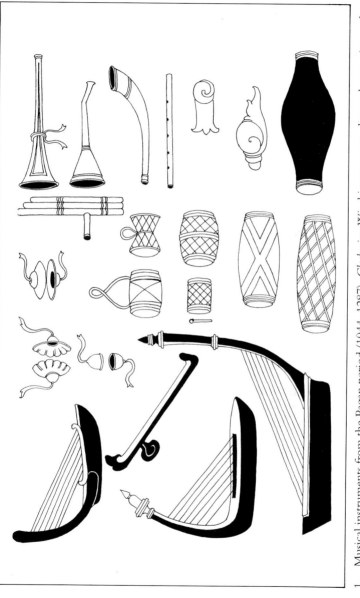

1. Musical instruments from the Pagan period (1044–1287). *Clockwise*: Wind instruments, drums, harps, *vina*, and cymbals.

and bronze frog-drums (Plate 1). Dancers are portrayed performing accompanied by a single instrument or by an ensemble.

At Pagan, inscriptions from the twelfth century mention the Mon word *pantara*. Among the Burmese, it became the collective term for dancers and singers, the former being known as *ka-che-the*, and the latter as *thi-chin-the* (Plate 2). Those taking part in a performance beautified their faces with a powder obtained from aromatic woods, and accentuated their eyes and eyebrows with Indian kohl eyeliner.

Judging by incidents mentioned in the *Hman-nan Maha Yazawindawgyi* [Glass Palace Chronicle] (1967), during the reigns of Narathu (1165?–74) and Narapatisithu (1174–1211), there were already professional troupes for hire, and some of the performances at court were designed to exploit the seductive charms of the young female dancers. In one instance, this led to the downfall of an elderly monk from Ceylon named Rahula, who was attending an alms-giving ceremony at the palace. He became obsessed with one of the court dancers and had to leave the Order. Prevented from remaining in the country, he carried the girl off to Malayu (Malaysia).

While the Burmese continued to enjoy the performing arts, in the north, Yunnan had fallen to the Mongol hordes of Kublai Khan, who also demanded a tribute from Pagan. This demand was ignored, and in 1287, the Mongols descended to the Irrawaddy plains, ending one of the most culturally progressive periods in Burmese history.

The Mongol invasion left its mark, for the songs and dances of the late thirteenth and fourteenth centuries were martial in nature. Dancing with weapons became popular, especially the *kar-ah-ka* (dance of the shield), which involved a sequence of defensive postures, and was performed to the accompaniment of gongs and cymbals. Thihathu (r. 1312–24) was a renowned exponent of this type of display, and his soldiers even had their arms tattooed with a picture of him dancing. His son Ngaseshin (r. 1343–50) was also an expert, and wrote *kar-chin* (shield songs) which have survived.

The *Twinthin Myanmar Yazawinthit* (1968) noted that at the festivities held at the Tupayon Pagoda, Sagaing, in 1466, there were

2.   A prince of Pagan being entertained by a singer and accompanist with
     tiny bells (*foreground*). Ananda Temple (1091), Pagan.

dancers from the ethnic minorities as well as strolling players from China, India, Ceylon, Thailand, and Viengchang. However, it is not clear whether the entertainers had come especially for the occasion, or whether they were from the various foreign communities who had settled in the country.

We learn from *Buridat-lingagyipyo*, a poem by the monk Ratthasara (1468–1529), based on the *Bhuridatta Jataka*, that the art of puppetry was well established by 1484. In another poem, *Than-wa-ya-pyo*, he described the city of Ah Wa (Ava) at night, and said that in the well-lit marionette shows, the dolls danced and performed acrobatic feats. Young men took part in shield dance displays, and harps and reed pipes could be heard accompanying melodious voices (Plate 3).

At the dedication ceremony of the Mingalazedi Pagoda at Tadar U in 1496, the pageants included decorated carriages, moving wooden figures, and singing maidens. Other entertainments were held in a huge building for the vast crowds which are said to have come from the 'four directions'.

In another poem, *Taung-tair-tun*, Ratthasara described the dancing girls, noting that they tinted their fingertips red with *dan* or henna (*Lawsonia* sp.) and made up their faces with powder obtained from sweet-smelling herbs and scented woods. They wore breast-cloths which were wrapped in a provocative manner, and secured by broad, jewelled gold belts. As their shimmering golden costumes were stored in boxes of scented wood, a wonderful fragrance filled the room when they danced.

An infusion of new styles enhanced Burmese dance further when Bayinnaung (r. 1551–81) sacked the city of Ayutthaya in 1567. He returned with the entire court, treasure, artisans, and entertainers. Pegu, his capital, was very cosmopolitan, and in its day people had the opportunity of hearing music and seeing dancers from places as far apart as Manipur and Thailand. Soon after his death, the great empire broke up, and one of his sons, Nyaungyan Min (r. 1599–1605), rebuilt the old city of Ah Wa and founded a new dynasty, which was to last until 1752.

Despite some unsettled times during this dynasty, a clearer picture of the performing arts begins to emerge. This is, in part,

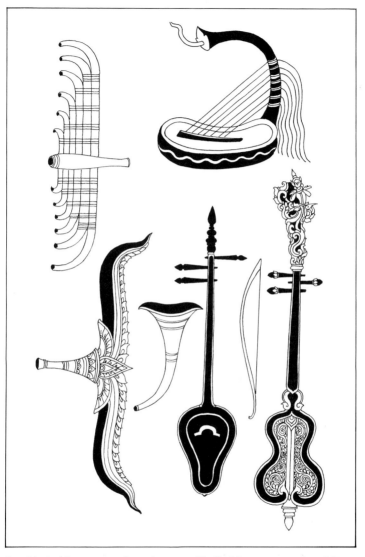

3. Musical instruments from the second half of the seventeenth and first half of the eighteenth centuries. *Clockwise*: Harp, violins, trumpet, and two decorated reed pipes.

due to the large volume of contemporary records and literature which have survived.

The collective term for singing, dancing, and playing music continued to be *pantara* until well into the seventeenth century. However, the new word *thabin* was gradually replacing it. Actors and dancers came to be known as *thabin-the*; the word *daw* (royal) was added to distinguish the court performers—*thabin-daw*.

According to a royal order issued by Anaukpetlun (r. 1605–28) in 1607, the palace entertainers were divided into nine *ah-su* (groups) known as:

1. *Se-daw ah-su*: Men who played the large royal drums.

2. *Pattha ah-su*: Those who played a variety of smaller drums.

3. *Pantara ah-su*: Male and female dancers, and play–actors.

4. *Khwet-khwin ah-su*: Brass instrument/cymbal players, etc.

5. *Gyun-khayar-pontaung ah-su*: Acrobats, trumpeters, players of another variety of small drum.

6. *Tha-nyar-the ah-su*: *Kinnari* (half-human, half-bird) dancers, who were also required to sing the different types of classical songs.

7. *Yodayar, Mon, Myanmar saing ah-su*: Thai, Mon, and Burmese orchestras.

8. *Ah-nyeint ah-su*: Dancers and musicians who were not part of the state troupe, but entertained in the private apartments of the king and his senior queens.

9. *Shaydawpyai ah-su*: Attendants who preceded the king in state processions; some danced, while others played instruments.

The order also set down rules concerning marriage between the entertainers and those outside their profession. It stated that a male child of the union had to follow his father's trade, while a female became one of the drummers of the chief queen.

It was inevitable that male members of the royal family often became involved with the dancers. Anaukpetlun, concerned for the purity of the dynasty, issued an order stating that the children of such liaisons were not to be registered as members of the royal family, but must either become court entertainers, or enter other court services.

In 1635, a great festival was held to celebrate the completion of a new palace at Ah Wa, built by Thalun (r. 1629–48). Men beat the royal drums at each of the nine inner city gates, and dancers performed. At court, intrigues between the dancers and princes were again on the increase, for Thalun was obliged to reissue Anaukpetlun's order of 1607, emphasizing that offspring of such unions would not be accepted as royalty.

During Thalun's reign, the state ceremonies and pagoda festivals continued to be accompanied by performances of all kinds. In 1637, after the guardian spirits of the palace had been propitiated, a large number of dancers, including Arakanese, Burmese, Chinese, Mon, and Thai, entertained.

The Rajamanisula Pagoda Inscription of 1649 noted that at the royal dedicatory celebrations, the dancers, dressed as *kinnari*, danced on a *lun-tin* (tightrope) and looked as if they were flying (Plate 4). This negates previous statements that only puppets were allowed to perform on a level higher than the audience. As human performers were considered socially inferior to the audience, it would have been offensive for them to occupy a position above the heads of the audience, who sat on the ground. Either this ruling did not exist in the 1640s, or perhaps exemption was granted for the *kinnari* dancers, who were probably members of the court troupe, as they were extravagantly dressed and adorned with expensive ornaments. The performance was no doubt organized by an official responsible for entertainments within the palace. A royal order of 1654 gives the earliest known title for this post as the Thabin Sayae (Clerk for the Performing Arts).

During the early 1700s, some of the rules regarding the status of court entertainers were relaxed, for one of the royal orders of Taninganway (r. 1714–33), dated 1715, said that the court dancer whom the king's uncle had married was to be accorded all the privileges due to her new rank, including the use of gold regalia. Nevertheless, such recognition was enjoyed by only a few. A girl with a 'reputation' would certainly have been barred.

It was during the reign of Mahadhammaraja Dipati (1733–52) that the first documented play, *Maniket*, by the minister Padaythayaza (1684–1752), was performed. The king, who was a keen astrologer, proclaimed that the end of his dynasty was at hand, and feeling powerless to interfere with fate, immersed himself in

4. A *kinnari* dancer performing on a *lun-tin* (tightrope) in 1649. Drawing by the author based on a woodcarving in the Phowintaung Caves, Monywa, Upper Burma, seventeenth century.

distractions. While entertainments were held nightly in the city, the countryside subsided into anarchy. Sensing an easy victory, the Mon ruler of Pegu seized the capital, now called Inn Wa, in 1752.

The Mon incursion into the Burmese heartland did not last, for Aung Zeya, headman of Shwebo, fought off the invaders and declared himself king. As Alaungphaya (r. 1752–60), he founded the Konbaung Dynasty (1752–1885). In 1755, Captain Baker, who was heading a mission from the East India Company to Shwebo, noted that there were 'several bands of various sorts of musick, and women dancers, unto the steps ascending the Presence Room'. Until the end of the dynasty in 1885, the Konbaung kings continued the tradition of maintaining entertainers, who were always present on ceremonial occasions.

Myedu Min (r. 1763–76) moved the capital back to Inn Wa in 1766, and sacked Ayutthaya the following year, taking thousands of captives. He later assigned the best craftsmen to the palace workshops. The performing arts of the Burmese, too, were further improved by Thai court dancers and musicians; the style called *yodayar* (Ayutthaya) is still equated with refinement. Although the court had been familiar with Thai dance forms since the fifteenth century, the new movements from Ayutthaya must have been of a superlative quality, as they became extremely popular. The *yodayar* was considered superior to the indigenous style, and aspiring dancers were obliged to master the movements if they wished to rise in their profession.

The dance was divided into twelve sections, six of which were considered refined and were danced in a stately manner by the principals. Characters such as the monkeys and the demons were assigned the robust movements. Trainees in the former type were taught not to hold the body rigid, but to move in an effortless manner 'as if there were no bones in the body'. Their posture had to be grand and their faces mask-like. The poses struck by the dancers delighted the Burmese, who felt that the elegant deportment personified the dignity of the court (Maung Htin Aung, 1937).

When excerpts from Thai plays such as *Enaung* and the *Ramayana* were performed, the captive Thai actors were allowed to appear in their national costumes. Although change of any kind was objected to by those in authority, the female dancers gradually adopted the indigenous style. Among the men's costumes, the Thai style continued, with modifications.

Soon after 1767, the Thai actor who played the role of Rama was given the Burmese name of Maung Mya. He was succeeded by Maung Po Way and Maung Po. Maung Hlaing was the first actor to appear as the hero Enaung in the play of the same name. Some of his dances involved the use of ornamental fingernails of metal, which were clicked in time to the music.

It was said that when Singu Min (r. 1776–82) was intoxicated, he would put on a mask and join the players, oblivious of the embarrassed murmurs from his courtiers. Towards the end of his reign, his chief queen, Thakin Min Mi, composed songs for the *Ramayana*.

By the 1770s, the word *thabin* had become established as the collective term for music, singing, dancing, and puppet shows, and was divided into three categories:

1. *Ahmyint-thabin*: Puppetry, where the use of a stage was allowed. As the puppeteers, who were also considered socially inferior, were hidden by a curtain they did not pose a threat to the 'dignity' of the audience.

2. *Ahneint-thabin*: Live performers who were considered socially inferior. Presentation was usually at ground level, not on a stage.

3. *Ah-nyeint-thabin*: Female entertainers who performed chiefly in the private apartments of the royal family.

Singu Min raised the rank of the Thabin Sayae (Clerk for the Performing Arts) to that of a Wun (Minister), an indication of increased responsibilities. Seven Thabin Wun were to hold this post between 1776 and 1885.

Many writers, including the present author, have been led to believe by articles published between 1950 and 1980, that the first Thabin Wun compiled a list of rules for the theatrical profession. However, Dr Than Tun in his work, *The Royal Orders of Burma*, is of the opinion that these regulations could be forgeries. The works, quoted in good faith, claimed that a Thabin Wun had to be proficient in all aspects of the entertainers' arts, and have knowledge of woodcarving, astrology, medicine, magic, religious and secular literature, and judicial and religious laws. He was also invested with power over all who were connected with his department.

In 1778, Singu Min celebrated the dedication ceremony of a monastery with acrobatic displays, martial arts, decorated carts, and dancers performing on taut lengths of cane. At night, fireworks and huge pyramids of oil-lamps lit the sky. The Pyi-gyi-thabin (Theatre of the Great Country), presumably the court troupe, staged the play *Aeinyananthi*. Large, richly dressed marionettes were also to be seen.

Badon Min's reign (1782–1819) saw a further rise in the quality of the performing arts (Colour Plate 2). This was largely due to Shwetaung Min (1762–1808), the Crown Prince, who took an interest in such matters. In 1785, he sent a mission to Laos, Thailand, Cambodia, and Java to record the dances, music, and plays of these kingdoms. Work on translating the acquired material was said to have begun in 1789, and the results contributed to the enrichment of the theatrical standards at court. Fifty-four volumes of the findings have survived, and are now preserved in the university at Mandalay.

While the Burmese appreciated the controlled movements of a dancer, some European visitors found them incomprehensible. Vincentius Sangermano (1893), an Italian priest, said that when dancing 'both men and women, moving slowly round the place of the entertainment, exhibit continual contortions with their bodies, their hands, and their fingers'. He revealed that the first time he saw Burmese dancers, he took them to be madmen.

On the other hand, Michael Symes (1800), a British envoy who witnessed a performance of the *Ramayana* at Pegu in 1795, found the dancers delightful, and dressed in 'showy and becoming' costumes. Symes considered that the play was better than any Indian drama he had seen. He was told that the best actors were 'natives of Siam'. This could imply that either the players were descendants of some of the captives of Ayutthaya, or that Thai troupes were again moving freely between the two kingdoms. When Symes visited the nobility, he found entertainers in the compounds surrounding their residences. At the palace of the Prince of Prome, elegant ladies performed in the galleries.

13

The Abbot of Monywai (1766–1835), writing about a court dancer in the early 1800s, said that she was proficient in the sixty-four dance postures, which she performed on a tightrope. He noted that she was extremely supple, and her movements so exquisite that the 'watching eyes became dizzy'.

Hiram Cox (1821), another British envoy who arrived in Rangoon in 1796, saw several bands of Thai dancers. He observed that 'some were gaudily dressed, as females, in velvet brocade with gold ornaments; the dancing consisted of various attitudes, and beating time to a slow measure with their feet'.

During Symes's second visit in 1802, he was entertained by a famous blind violinist. This performance was held outside the palace stockade, for 'a strong prejudice appears to run against all natural deformities', and blind persons, no matter how talented, were 'forbidden to enter the Palace enclosure' (Hall, 1955).

Another set of rules for the entertainment profession was allegedly drawn up during the reign of Sagaing Min (1819–37) by his Thabin Wun. However, Dr Than Tun also considers these to be forgeries. John Crawfurd (1829), who visited the court in 1827, found the music trying. He mentions a 'celebrated' but disreputable actor called Maung Shwe Nyan, who was the king's favourite, and was seen wearing the 'highest chain of nobility given to a subject'. Despite strong prejudice and the saying 'actors and beggars, eaters of food to be thrown away', at least one was ennobled and forced to be accepted by the court. Crawfurd also met the Thabin Wun, an elderly Thai, who was known as the Minister for Marionettes and Drama.

Some of the songwriters of this reign, such as Myawaddy Wungyi U Sa (1766–1853), borrowed musical themes not only from the Karen, Mon, and Thai, but also from the choral music of the Christian mercenaries.

Mindon Min (r. 1853–78) moved the capital to Mandalay in 1857, and although his benign rule attracted leading exponents of the performing arts, the religiously inclined king favoured puppet shows over the live theatre. The former tended to specialize in the *Jataka Tales* (birth stories of the Buddha), whereas the latter portrayed romantic plays, such as the *Ramayana*, still admired by the court.

On the demise of the king in 1878, a palace clique placed the weak Theebaw (r. 1878–85) on the throne. Afraid to leave his stockaded palace, the king and his domineering queen, Suphayarlat, indulged in extravagant and novel forms of entertainment. Despite the incompetence and cruelty of this reign, it was a time when the performing arts came into their own in a spectacular way. It was, indeed, a time of plenty for the performers, and within the walled city music could be heard nightly from the shows taking place in its numerous streets.

2

Court Musicians of the
Konbaung Dynasty, 1752–1885

MUSICIANS who served in the palace were registered as *ahmu-htan* (crown service personnel), and were divided into two groups, those who provided background music for the daily ceremonies, and those who entertained. Outstanding individuals were rewarded with minor titles and lands. Yet curiously, by the second half of the eighteenth century, musicians were placed in the same social class as executioners (Trager and Koenig, 1979).

The Burmese court realized that music was a powerful accompaniment to ceremonies and, since the days of the kings of Pagan, had employed *se-gyi-pantra* (dancers of the big drums) to play the royal drums at audiences. The sovereign's authority and dignity were thought to be enhanced by the booming sound of these drums.

It was also believed from the earliest times that drums made from a particular type of wood could be ritually prepared with spells for warding off threats from enemies. Such drums were beaten facing the direction from which the attack was expected. On annexing a state, the court drums of the vanquished were ceremonially perforated by the conqueror. This was claimed to nullify whatever occult power was inherent in them. Thus, because of their supposed properties, drums were to become the premier musical instrument, not only for the ceremonies of the Burmese kings, but also among the common people.

The ritualized lives of palace residents revolved around the beating of a huge drum called the *baho-se*, and a triangular gong, which indicated the time. By the sixteenth century, it had become obligatory at the beginning of each reign to renew not only the time-drum, but also the drums used during audiences, those which announced the monarch's departure and return to his capital, and the drums at the four main city gates. Old drums were left in the precincts of a royal pagoda and allowed to decay.

Although the royal drums were adopted by succeeding dynasties, detailed information concerning their use after the fall of Pagan has so far been found only in records from the eighteenth century.

A royal order for 1755 indicates that a large number of musical instruments was used at the inception of the Konbaung Dynasty in 1752. Later accounts show that the number decreased during successive reigns. The order listed twelve large drums, a pair of conches, four large horns, four small horns, four elongated horns, two trumpets, two large silver trumpets, four small silver trumpets, four clarinets, three Mon oboes, a pair of clappers, and cymbals. By the 1850s, the royal drums were only accompanied by one small drum and cymbals.

In the audience hall, two pairs of drums, known as the Appearance and the Withdrawal Drums, were hung on stands. The former were beaten to announce the approach of the royal couple, as they mounted the steps from the back of the gilded hour-glass shaped throne, which was 180 centimetres high, and stopped when they sat down on its flat surface, facing the courtiers crouched below them. The audience ended when a silver gong was struck, followed by the beating of the Withdrawal Drums. On duty, a drummer wore a long *pasoe* (sarong) and a flowing white jacket (Plate 5). In the 1870s, thirty-four royal drummers were listed as being employed at the Mandalay court.

When the monarch went on tour, he was accompanied by five auspicious drums. Each bore a name; one was called Pyi-lon-noe (wake the whole country). Other instruments included a gong of solid gold, and a special drum used by his subjects when they wished to attract his attention to report a grievance.

All court musicians were restricted from performing outside the palace, except at royal functions, or with special permission from the king. At the end of an event, they had to return instruments made from precious metals to the Treasury.

The duties of the entertainment musicians involved playing during celebrations, religious ceremonies, processional music for pageants and regattas, and overtures and incidental music for the court theatrical performances, including marionette shows.

5. The royal *se-daw* drums of King Theebaw being played for the last time during the visit of Lord Dufferin to the Mandalay palace in 1886. From *The Graphic*, March 1886.

Another group of musicians, an all-female troupe, performed mainly in the king's private apartments, and were registered as *ah-nyeint-ahpyodaw* (maids of honour who provide genteel entertainment). Its members were trained not only to play music, but to recite poetry, sing, dance, and act. On state occasions, foreign dignitaries who witnessed this type of entertainment noted that the female players were always dressed in fantastic robes.

There were also small specialist orchestras which did not come under the jurisdiction of the Thabin Wun, but under that of an official called the Nat-htein (Guardian of the Spirits), who was responsible for propitiation ceremonies. These divinities were housed in numerous shrines within the palace, near the city walls and gates.

Lowest in the hierarchy of musicians was a group which played at the funerals of members of the royal family and courtiers. Being considered 'unclean', they were forbidden to enter the palace complex.

A full orchestra of the type which entertained was called a *saing-waing*, and consisted of drums and percussion and wind instruments. The *saing-daw-gyi*, or state orchestra, was employed on great ceremonial occasions within the royal theatre. Next in grade were the Orchestras of the Royal Left and the Royal Right (musicians from the latter were more senior in rank). The *ah-twin-saing-daw* (orchestra of the inner palace), like the troupe of female musicians, provided music for more intimate occasions. These grades were possibly introduced during the reign of Badon Min by Shwetaung Min, the Crown Prince, as little information is available for the periods before 1782.

The most prominent item in an orchestra was the *pat-waing*, a circular wooden frame containing twelve double-headed drums, graduating in size. The musicians took their cue from the player, who was also leader of the orchestra. It is known that in 1785 the man who headed the Orchestra of the Royal Left was Nga Tayoke; his name appears again in 1805, indicating that talented individuals enjoyed a long career. Although this instrument was considered the preserve of males, the author has a lacquer box from the 1820s which shows a female playing the *pat-waing* before the king.

Many of the instruments, such as the drums, were made within the city, while those of a more complicated nature, like the elaborate harps and the wind and percussion instruments, were produced in the palace workshops. The royal smithy was responsible for the gongs of various sizes which were struck during battle, and were played for entertainment; brass was used for the former, and silver for the latter. Senior ministers and members of the royal family were allocated trumpets of silver for use in state processions.

It would appear that until 1787, harps, oboes, and xylophones were decorated with glass mosaic and gilding, and were used indiscriminately by all ranks. In that year, the Crown Prince ordered their confiscation. Henceforth, only the court musicians and troupes belonging to the Crown Prince and other senior princes enjoyed this privilege. The Crown Prince also reorganized the court entertainers, and exempted trainee musicians from palace duties.

In the early 1880s, three new orchestras were created. These were known as the Diamond, Emerald, and Ruby Orchestras after their instruments which were decorated in white, green, and red glass mosaic set in gilt. The lead musicians were allocated the prestigious *thaing* (gilded cane wand), four of which were inserted in the wooden panels of the drum-circle. The percussionist who played the gong-circle was allowed two.

Another variation of the gilded wand was the *thaing-alan-phyu* (wand with white flag). However, as court paintings prior to the reign of Theebaw do not include these symbols when depicting the palace orchestras, they may have been introduced only during his reign.

Dagon Khin Khin Lay (1954) has noted that in the 'olden days' (period unclear) musical instruments were listed under five headings:

1. *Kye* (brass): Small bells, cymbals, and gongs.

2. *Kyo* (string): Harps, violins, and zithers.

3. *Tha-ye* (leather): A variety of drums.

4. *Lay* (wind): Flutes, oboes, and trumpets. Another list claimed that there were eight types of wind instruments, all under the heading of *tan-po*, but failed to offer details.

5. *Let-khok* (clapper): A length of bamboo split half-way down

the middle; there were also wooden clappers.

The instruments used by some of the maids of honour were the violin, xylophone, reed pipe, flute, curved harp, crocodile-shaped harp, tiny bells, small drum, and wooden clappers.

A player of a stringed instrument entered the presence of the king, or members of the royal family, with an assistant carrying a duplicate, as it was considered a sign of ill-omen if one of the strings snapped during a performance; it was, in fact, a punishable offence. The damaged instrument had to be withdrawn quickly, and a new one substituted. This superstition was extended to the marionette theatre, where great care had to be taken to ensure that no mishaps occurred during a royal performance.

Records for the Mandalay period (1857–85) list 133 court musicians, who were paid monthly and also given ricefields. The lists do not include those who performed chamber music, the female drummers, or the large number of small orchestras which were employed in propitiating the spirits guarding the palace complex and the city.

3
Theatricals at Court

DURING the Konbaung period (1752–1885), the premier events within the palace were the homage days held in April, August, and November, when the officials of the realm came to the capital to renew their allegiance to the king. Following the ceremony, the dignitaries were entertained for three nights with marionette shows, dances, music, and plays, which were of a quality only to be experienced at court.

Although it is not yet known when plays were first staged within the palace, one writer has claimed that during the late fifteenth and early sixteenth centuries, poems such as *Buridat-zatpaungpyo* (*Bhuridatta Jataka*) and *Hatthipala-zat* (*Hatthipala Jataka*) by the monk Ratthasara were meant to be either read or performed (Maung Khin Min, 1976). Thereafter, there was a gap of more than two centuries before the first documented court play, *Maniket*, was produced in 1733. It is stated that the playwright had given stage and musical instructions, and that for the first time songs were sung at the end of each scene (Ba Han, 1966). This would suggest that before *Maniket* there were other plays in which there was only spoken dialogue.

Although *Maniket* was an adaptation of the Thai *Thatta-danu*, it was once thought that Thai plays were first enacted within the palace only after 1767, by the court troupe from Ayutthaya. However, as was noted in Chapter 1, the presence of dancers from Thailand was recorded from as early as 1466. It is unlikely that the Burmese court did not know some of the Thai plays performed from that time onwards.

During the reign of Alaungphaya (1752–60), an official named Shwetaung Thihathu wrote a play called *Yadana-kyai-mon* [The Jewelled Mirror], which was said to have differed in style from the usual type of play, implying that there were others. One account claimed that the play was meant to be read and not performed.

Since the printing press was unknown at the time, and if the work was to be circulated, copies would have had to be laboriously written on palm-leaves (*Myanmar Swairson Kyam* (*Encyclopedia Birmanica*), 1954–76). On the other hand, the play was possibly read or recited before an audience by a *kwetseik saya* (story-teller). Until the 1960s, such performances were accompanied by an orchestra to provide background music, and to indicate a change of scene.

After the conquest of Ayutthaya in 1767, plays such as *Enaung* and the *Ramayana* came to dominate the court theatre because of the novelty of presentation. Evidence from works of art and inscriptions of the Pagan period indicates that the adventures of Rama were known to the Burmese from an early date. In 1973, two seventeenth-century palm-leaf manuscripts entitled *Yama-wutthu* [The Story of Rama] were discovered. Before this, most writers had believed that the epic was introduced from Thailand in 1767. However, Ono Toru (1993) has pointed out that the Burmese version of the *Ramayana* was not based on either the Thai *Ramakien* or the *Hikayat Sri Rama* of Malaysia. He noted that it followed, with slight variations, the original story of Valmiki, implying that it was acquired direct from India.

The oldest known work in play form to have survived is *Thiri Yama* [Sri Rama] from the late eighteenth or early nineteenth century. In 1775, a collection of songs based on the epic was composed, and survives in the *Yama Thargyin* [Songs from the *Ramayana*]. These were followed, during the reign of Singu Min (1776–82), by the songs of his queen, Thakin Min Mi. In 1789, the Crown Prince ordered U Sa to prepare new songs and musical preludes for the *Ramayana* and other Thai plays.

When the *Ramayana* was performed in its entirety, it took forty-five nights, according to one source, while another said sixty-five; no dates are offered. These marathon performances were probably held on extremely rare occasions. Pictorial evidence suggests that there were two types of presentation. Sometimes the humans, apart from the fanciful characters, appeared without masks. A second version showed almost all the players to be masked in the tradition of the *khon* drama of Ayutthaya (Colour Plate 3). During

23

a performance, the actor either tilted back the mask to speak, or mimed to the voice of a person seated at the back.

Masks from the epic were made of papier mâché, and ornamented with glass fragments and gilt. Those that represented the heroes were stored separately from those of the villains, and each group of players kept to their own area backstage. When not in use, the masks were placed on altars, with offerings of flowers for the spirit of the character which resided within each. Unfortunately, none of the masks used by the court troupes has survived; they can be seen only in paintings from the second half of the nineteenth century.

The second play which rivalled the *Ramayana* in popularity was originally called *Aindarwuntha*, but was later changed to *Enaung* (Colour Plate 4). Attempts to translate the entire play into Burmese began in 1798, but remained unfinished when the Crown Prince died in 1808. His son, Sagaing Min, ordered Myawaddy Wungyi U Sa to complete the work; one account claims that it was finished only in 1829. The *Mahagita* [Book of Songs] (1954) reports that during the reign of Tharrawaddy Min (1837–46), Myawaddy Wungyi U Sa rewrote the play and added new songs. A full performance was said to have taken from one and a half to two months but this, too, must have been on rare occasions.

A third play which was popular was *Thudanu* (*Manawhari*) or *Dway Mai Naw*. This was a Burmese version of one of the dramas based on a cycle of twelve plays around the legendary Indonesian hero, Pandji. The popularity of the story in Burma can be judged from the fact that the people of the Kayah State have claimed the heroine, Dway Mai Naw, as their own, and point to a prominent peak, called Ngwe-taung (Silver Hill), as the site of her fairy kingdom. The story centred around a *kinnari* princess, and was one of the first plays to be translated into English, as *The Silver Hill*, in 1856.

During the Konbaung period, many of the dramatists were members of the royal family and courtiers. Although others flourished outside palace circles, the benefits of royal patronage soon drew them to the capital. Dagon Nat Shin, writing in the 1950s, considers that the two men responsible for the rise in

24

the standard of the theatre were Myawaddy Wungyi U Sa and the Prince of Pyinsi. Performances were designed to gratify the eyes and ears, and produce a feeling of well-being.

A list of plays from the nineteenth century contains over a hundred titles, many of which had been written for the court puppet theatre, but were also performed by actors.

The title of a play which was written for performance at court was prefixed with the words *nan-dwin* (within the palace); the word *zat* (story) was added after the titles of plays for the common people. As the number of plays increased during the second half of the nineteenth century, it was found necessary to distinguish them as follows:

1. *Nibatwin Mahawin zat*: Based on the birth stories of the Buddha, which were popular with the pious.

2. *Phaya-thamaing*: Historical or fictional accounts of pagodas, concerning miracles, treasure, and ghosts.

3. *Yazawin zat*: Biographies of historical personalities.

4. *Dandaye*: Folk-tales about animals, myths, and magic.

5. *Hto zat*: Fiction.

While some plays were based on incidents which occurred in Burma, others were set in an ancient Indian city, the most popular being Benares (Varanasi). As the plots centred on the former lives of the Buddha, the leading characters had to be male, which gave actors precedence over actresses. At the time, women were considered inferior, and were not even allowed on to a puppet stage, which meant that all the female roles in such performances had to be sung by men.

Court dramatists, such as U Kyin U (1819–53) and U Ponnya (1807–66), were often persuaded to produce works with a 'message' on matters important at the time. When U Ponnya's play, *Paduma*, which featured a lecherous and murderous heroine, was staged, the court ladies became concerned that menfolk would see them in the same light. To repair the damage, U Ponnya was cajoled into writing what was to become one of his best-known works, *Wey-than-daya zat* (*Vessantara Jataka*), which featured the virtuous Madi. When some of Mindon Min's sons became troublesome, U Ponnya was asked to write the play *Wi-za-ya* [The Story of Prince Vijayo of Ceylon], a turbulent prince who was driven out of the kingdom by his father. The warning, however, was not heeded by the princes, and in the rebellion of 1866 many were killed. U Ponnya was found to be an accessory, and was secretly put to death.

Within the palace, plays were always performed when major festivals, nuptials, and other ceremonies connected with the numerous royal offspring were celebrated (Plate 6). To accommodate the crowds, a temporary theatre, which might consist of either one or several structures, was built near the main audience hall (Plate 7). On occasions, some of the state apartments were used. Other entertainments could be enjoyed on the small pavilions dotted along the main avenues.

There was also a permanent building, known as the Pwe-kyi-saung (theatre pavilion), which was, by tradition, built close to the queen mother's apartment (Plate 8). A *hti-yon-daw* (umbrella-shaped structure) was erected opposite the Pwe-kyi-saung. An enormous central pillar was the only part of this performing area which was left permanently fixed. The conical roof of bamboo matting, which was about 15 metres wide, was covered with cloth held down by a trellis. Around this column, at ground level, drama and dancing displays were presented. The courtiers were seated on carpets, the men on the left, and the ladies on the right.

Possibly the earliest picture of a *hti-yon-daw* can be seen in the *Burney Parabaik*, a manuscript from the early part of the nineteenth century, which is now in the British Library. In one scene, bananas are shown hanging from the rafters. These were for the players, who were allowed to refresh themselves during the performance, which lasted all night.

A Western-style theatre building, with a stage, first appeared in Burma during the Second Anglo-Burmese War of 1852. It was constructed by the British military authorities on the upper terrace of the Shwe Dagon Pagoda in Rangoon, for the entertainment of army personnel. No doubt, other theatres were built when Lower Burma was annexed by the British in 1853, and Rangoon became the capital of British Burma. Theatrical companies from England

6. Theatricals at court. Painting by the author based on a scene in the Sulamani Temple, Pagan, second half of the eighteenth century.

7. A performance in the *hti-yon-daw* (umbrella-shaped structure) at the
   Mandalay palace. Wall-painting in the Shwe Gu Nee Pagoda,
   Kyaukkar, Monywa, *c.*1880.

8. The Mandalay palace, with the royal theatre on the left. From the *Illustrated London News*, May 1886.

are known to have given performances in the city. Such Western-style theatre buildings were to influence the Burmese entertainment profession, and by the early 1880s their use had been adopted within the Mandalay palace.

Laurie (1880), in his *Our Burmese Wars*, reported that Theebaw's Italian engineers had invented a machine for rocking the royal cradle. As the two theatres at the Mandalay court had moving scenery and trapdoors, and were capable of showing flying chariots and lotus flowers opening to reveal dancers, one wonders if the Italians, with their noted fondness for the theatre, had an influence on these properties.

The two theatres, erected in 1884 as part of the celebrations following the ear-piercing ceremony of Theebaw's daughter, were sited in the eastern and western sectors of the palace compound, and were appropriately called the Ahshay and Ahnauk Zat Yondawgyi (Eastern and Western Theatres). The *Ramayana*, with its scenes of battle, was enacted in the former for the male members of the court. In the latter, situated in the women's quarter, the play *Enaung*, with its love intrigues, delighted the ladies. Small elephants and ponies were said to have been used to draw carriages ridden by some of the characters. The festivities and performances are known to have lasted three months (U Tin, 1967).

A painting of the Eastern Theatre which appeared in *The Magazine of Art* (1891–2) shows Theebaw and his court watching a play being performed under the traditional umbrella structure (Plate 9). Behind this can also be seen a raised stage decorated with painted panels, flanked by two doorways at ground level. The actors appeared from one door to perform in the umbrella area, and then made their exit through the other door. For episodes in which mechanical devices were required, the scene shifted to the stage.

Records for the reign claim that vast amounts of money were spent on the entertainments, and that during one year the production costs for the *Ramayana* alone were 25,000 kyats. The cast involved over 200 actors and four orchestras. Theebaw's queen, Suphayarlat, was lavish with her gifts to the players, and would

9. The royal theatre, showing the traditional and Western-style structures. From *The Magazine of Art* (1891–2), London. (Courtesy of Patricia Herbert)

award a clown 1,000 kyats for telling a witty joke; at that time, a domestic servant had to feed her family on 3 kyats a month.

It was said that as the royal couple were indecisive about what they wished to see, a variety of entertainers were kept costumed and waiting in the wings. Occasionally, touring companies from France and India appeared at the Mandalay court. One of these, the Parsee Victoria Company, was invited back several times.

During the hot weather months, the king and queen would retire to a summer house in the palace gardens, and watch the actors perform excerpts from some of their favourite plays (Colour Plate 5).

4
Court Dancers and Other Performers

ACTORS and actresses who were employed within the palace of the Konbaung kings (1752–1885) were also expected to sing and dance. This was necessary, because before the stage with a drop-curtain was introduced in the early 1880s, most scenes, particularly in the Thai plays, ended with the characters making their exit by dancing their way back to the changing area behind the orchestra.

During the second half of the nineteenth century, performers at the very top of their profession were referred to as *nar-myi-ya*, meaning someone who had made a name for himself, and at the end of a display, received a reward from the royal family and dignitaries. It was to be expected that while one actor became renowned for his recitations, others became famous for their singing, or dancing, or the convincing portrayal of a character.

A player had to be educated, and a good memory was also essential, as much of the dialogue was lengthy and there were no prompters. In instances where lines were forgotten, actors had to improvise. The dialogue was usually in rhyme, and was either sung or recited. It was not composed in colloquial Burmese, but in the elegant style of the court. Each word had to be spoken with the correct emphasis, so that the musicians could take their cue and provide the appropriate accompaniment.

Prior to the adoption of the Western-style stage in the early 1880s, some incidents had to be described beforehand. Most plays contained distressing scenes in which characters were tortured by someone in authority; this enabled the actors or actresses to show off their ability to sing an emotional *ngo-chin* (weeping song). There was, however, very little action. An aggressor rarely attempted to go through the motions of beating a character; he would simply recite an appropriate verse with great feeling, warning his victim that he was about to feel the stinging lash of his cane. Assisted by loud music from the orchestra, the actor would roll on the floor in feigned agony.

During the mid-1800s, because of adverse conditions in the palace and the war with the British, the court theatre did not flourish for some years. A revival began only when Mindon Min moved the capital to Mandalay in 1857. Here, the Thai plays began to enjoy a revival, culminating in the grand displays which ended with the fall of the Konbaung Dynasty in 1885.

Although the court was entertained by many fine performers, only a handful of names are known. Each individual was to leave his or her mark on the style of presentation and the dance forms, which were copied by others in the profession.

In the 1860s, San Toke was famous for the role of Enaung, and for his unmatched performance of the *yodayar*. He was originally called Say Nee (Red Tattoo) San Toke, because of the magical designs tattooed in red ink on his body, which were believed to make him sexually attractive. In his youth, he is said to have suffered much from the attentions of the court ladies who showered him with gifts. For a time, this resulted in the king ordering him to cover his face when he entered the palace, as he was liable to be mobbed (Dagon Khin Khin Lay, 1954).

If the male lead appeared as a prince from one of the classical dramas, he wore a tapering *magaik* (crown), a tight-fitting, long-sleeved jacket called a *htaing-ma-thein-ein-gyi*, and a *pasoe* (sarong) tucked up between the legs, with the ends hanging at the back in a *kyet-mee* (rooster's tail). Around his neck was a *lair-char* (sequinned collar), while from his waist hung *bon* (curling panels) (Colour Plate 6). He carried either an ornamental bow or a sword. Many of the costumes for the court dancers, including those taking the role of the *kinnari* (half-bird, half-human) (Colour Plate 7), were produced by the tailors and embroiderers who made the robes of state.

A Thai actress, Hnin Nu (Delicate Mist), is listed as being one of the leading dancers during the 1790s. Yindaw Ma Lay, Sin Kho Ma Lay, and Ma Htway Lay were the most outstanding prima donnas during the period between 1860 and 1885, and are said to have added their distinctive styles to the traditional form of dancing at court.

Yindaw Ma Lay joined the élite company of *ah-nyeint-ahpyodaw* (maids of honour) during the late 1850s, and moved on to play lead-

ing roles such as Princess Phutsapar in *Enaung*. She was a superb
dancer and a coquette, and was a great favourite with the male
members of the court. When Theebaw became king, his queen,
Suphayarlat, favoured Yindaw's younger rival, Ma Shwe Hmyin
(b. 1852). This dancer, whose troupe had moved to Mandalay in 1874,
had caught the roving eye of the Prince of Yanaung, a notorious
reprobate, and an enemy of Suphayarlat. He ordered the dancer to
divorce her husband, and imperiously sent an official, riding an
elephant, to fetch her. The scandal circulated, and the people
nicknamed her Sin Kho Ma Lay (she who was carried off by
elephant). Witty craftsmen also immortalized the incident in wood
and clay (Plate 10).

The Prince of Yanaung was later murdered on Suphayarlat's orders,
and the dancer imprisoned and beaten. Later, the queen relented
and made her prima donna of the court troupe. However, royal
favouritism never lasted long. Sin Kho Ma Lay was soon replaced
by a descendant of Badon Min, called Ma Htway Lay (1867–1927),
who had been seduced at the age of twelve by the Prince of
Yanaung. At the time, the child had been famous for her imitation
of the difficult dance movements of a 'princess' marionette owned
by the court puppeteer, Saya Pu. During the reign of Theebaw,
due to the patronage of the powerful Queen Suphayarlat, the leading lady took precedence over the male lead.

When playing a princess, the female lead was dressed in a
sequinned robe composed of flame-like shapes. For other roles, she
wore a jacket, also called a *htaing-ma-thein-ein-gyi*. Unlike that worn
by the Mintha, it was open in front to reveal a *yin-se* (breast-cloth);
sometimes a *tabet* (shawl) was used. From about the 1880s,
necklaces called *mok padee* became fashionable; paintings of dancers
before that period show them wearing little jewellery. Around her
waist was wrapped a *htamein* skirt, the *ahnar* (tail) of which trailed
behind her. Her oiled hair was dressed in an elaborate knot and
ornamented with jewels and flowers.

When plays were not staged within the royal theatre, the king
was entertained by a troupe of *ah-nyeint-ahpyodaw*, who were picked
for their beauty, education, and expertise in singing, dancing, or
music. Many were born of liaisons between princes and dancing girls,

10. The dancer Sin Kho Ma Lay being carried
off by elephant. Needlework container of
wood, late nineteenth century.

and although never acknowledged as royalty, they were treated
with consideration. Once past their prime, the more gifted were
retained at court where they instructed the next generation of
ah-nyeint-ahpyodaw.

In 1878, thirty-one such performers were listed in three sections:
the *ah-shay* (eastern), *ah-twin* (inner), and *ah-nyauk* (western). The
definitions applied to the various quarters of the vast palace
platform which housed numerous state buildings, and in which
each group performed.

1. Pyu dancers, c. AD 800. Painting by the author based on terracotta plaques.

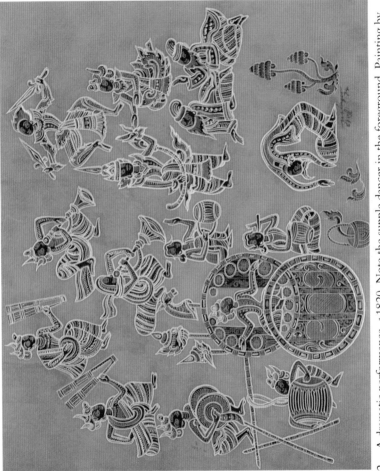

2. A dramatic performance, *c*.1820. Note the supple dancer in the foreground. Painting by the author based on a design from a lacquer box.

3. Lakshmana (gold mask), Sita, and Rama (green mask), court dancers as characters from the *Yama-zat* (*Ramayana*), *c*.1880. Painting by the author (1993).

4. Scenes from the court play *Enaung*. Painting for a fan, c.1890.

5.   The king and queen at a performance in the Mandalay palace gardens. Note the white flags on the drum-circle. Painting by the author (1994).

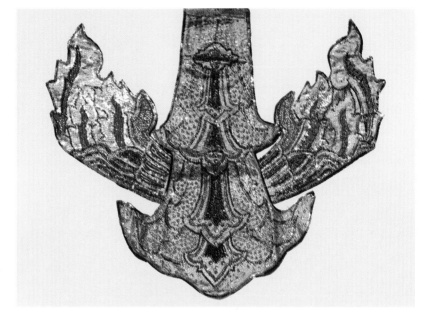

6. The front piece worn by a Mintha when performing the *yodayar* dance. Made by the author in the 1960s.

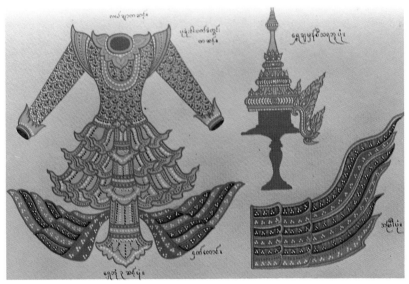

7. The costume of a *kinnari* dancer from the Mandalay palace. Design copied by the author from a nineteenth-century manuscript.

8. The procession of a wooden elephant, painted red, being carried around the royal compound in the *sin-khon-pwe*, c.1880. Painting from a manuscript.

9. An *ozi* drummer with a female cymbal player, 1993. (Courtesy of Sylvia Fraser-Lu)

10. A *bon-shay* (double-headed drum) group with two dancers. Painting on silk, c.1880.

11. Children performing a play, c.1900.

12. A *yein* (chorus) dance by a group of young girls at a Buddhist festival, c.1890s.

13. The dance of the *pin-taing-san* (crown princess), *c.*1900.

14. An *ah-nyeint* troupe performing in the street, c.1900. A spirit (*centre*) sends a tiger (*foreground*) to carry off the heroine who sits weaving (*right*).

15. The *ah-nyeint* Minthamee Ma Thein May as a Mintha (*left*) with the leading lady and a clown, *c.*1910.

16. U Sein Win, mask-maker for the Obo Nandwin Yama Troupe and other *Ramayana* companies in Rangoon, with demon masks, 1994. This troupe was founded during the late nineteenth century and performs annually.

17. The spirit 'palace' at Taungbyon, near Mandalay. Dancing mediums are with the orchestra on the platform, drunken revellers are below, c.1869. (Courtesy of the Trustees of the Victoria and Albert Museum)

There was also a troupe of female dancers and musicians known as the *Mon-ah-nyeint*, although among the numerous subjugated ethnic groups, only the Mon enjoyed this privilege. The highlights of the year for the different grades of *ah-nyeint-ahpyodaw* were at the three homage-paying ceremonies. On such occasions they performed for five days separately from the court troupe. Sometimes they danced at ceremonies connected with the royal children, and before the sacred white elephant. Accommodation for these entertainers was in a 'long house', said to have been located near the palace gardens. One of the earliest representations of this category of entertainers can be seen in the murals of the Ananda Okkyaung (1775) at Pagan (Plate 11).

The senior queens, princes, and princesses also retained their own small groups of female dancers.

There were others at court who, although they entertained on state and other festive occasions, were not considered *thabin-the* (belonging to the theatrical profession). These were the sons and daughters of the officials, who performed group dances. Their

11.   A female *ah-nyeint* singer and musicians at court. Wall-painting from the Ananda Okkyaung (1775), Pagan.

37

performances were very numerous, and sometimes took the form of imitating the peasantry with various displays of folk-dancing.

Some of the regiments staffed by descendants of captives from conquered kingdoms also provided dances from their native lands. During the early 1880s, even Chinese dragon dances were a familiar sight within the palace.

Among the younger male retainers, one of the more important and popular dances held every October was the procession of the *sin-khon-pwe* (elephant-hopping dance), which was first recorded in 1646, and which continued to be performed until 1885. Originally, four gilded wooden elephants were used, one by each of the four groups of palace guards, but by the nineteenth century several variations had evolved. It is not known why this particular animal was used.

When Thalun (r. 1629–48) built the Rajamanisula Pagoda at Sagaing, he ordered each of the four regiments guarding a quarter of the palace stockade to present a carving of an elephant. The figures were placed in shrines, and offerings made. During the day, the elephants, accompanied by music and dancing, were taken around the compounds of the Crown Prince and high officials. On the day of the full moon, the four figures were placed on gilded barges and taken as offerings to the pagoda (Thiri U Zana, 1962).

According to a record for 1805, the *sin-khon-pwe* had altered. The elephant was no longer gilded, but was painted red, and was the property of a prince. It was placed in a palanquin and taken around the compounds, accompanied by two dancers, a gong player, and a drummer; a variation appears in Colour Plate 8. The money collected at each residence was shared among those taking part. Later, the carving was returned to the prince and placed in his children's nursery, and not offered to a pagoda (U Tin, 1932–3).

During the Mandalay period (1857–85), several groups of young men circulated around the inner city carrying either red or gilded elephants in palanquins, accompanied by dancers and musicians (U Tin, 1967). In another variation for the same period, a group was led by a dancer dressed in a fantastic robe as the Hindu god Brahma. Carrying a gilded elephant, he hopped (*khon*), sang, and danced his way around the houses of royalty and officials. It also became a tradition, among the revellers, to hire a puppet troupe with the money collected (Maung Win Maung, 1972).

For the denizens of the Burmese court, a wide choice of entertainments thus existed, from the lavish court plays and marionette performances, to a variety of group dance displays.

5

Entertainment among the Common People
during the Nineteenth Century

SOME authorities on the theatre are of the opinion that the combined influences of the early rituals of the mediums, in which the stories of the spirits were enacted, and the *nebhatkhin* (a religious pageant of a minor birth story of Buddha) contributed to the evolution of drama (Maung Htin Aung, 1937; U Min Naing, 1959). In time, small troupes of strolling players emerged, while in some regions villagers developed a style known as drum dancing. Both troupes included music, song, dance, and a short play.

During the eighteenth century, combined efforts by breakaway groups among the drummers and some of the strolling players finally blossomed into full theatrical productions called *myai-waing*, or 'earth circling performances', as the action took place within a circular area formed by the audience seated around it. During the performance, the actors had no choice but to either dance or move in a circle in this restricted area to allow their faces to be seen.

Nebhatkhin

This simple type of entertainment possibly originated during the latter half of the Pagan period (1044–1287), with a monk relating to his congregation one of the 550 minor stories of the previous lives of the Buddha. The next logical step would have been for some elders, inspired by the tales, to organize a *nebhatkhin*, composed of young people from the locality. These pageants combined entertainment with religion, as visual instruction stood a better chance of being absorbed by the largely illiterate people. Although the inception of such shows has been tentatively assigned to 1531 (Maung Htin Aung, 1937), the present author is of the opinion that they were already in existence sometime before then.

In the early displays, presentation consisted of scenes containing motionless characters from one or several stories, with each set piece placed on a bullock cart. The vehicles congregated at a pagoda where the worshippers were gathered, and at a signal, such as the striking of a gong, those taking part would freeze in a pose. Later, the convoy of carts moved around the streets, stopping at sites along the way, and repeated the performance.

In time, dialogue, songs, and music were introduced to this silent, static form of entertainment. With these improvements, however, the caravan of carts required for a single story became redundant, as it could be replaced by one troupe acting the plot from beginning to end. Other organizers, however, continued with the traditional form of presenting mute, impassive characters. Thus, both types flourished side by side.

By the second half of the eighteenth century, the selection of stories to be staged had gravitated to the ten major *zat* (birth stories), for they had become better known than the 550 minor tales. This preference was also seen in the live theatre and the puppet shows, both at court and among the common people. However, even during the nineteenth century, the pageants continued to be called *nebhatkhin*, and not *zat-khin*.

Drum Dancing

At festival times, groups of young men roamed the streets, with their leader playing on an *ozi* (goblet-shaped drum), accompanied by a dancer. Emphasis was on the skill of the drummer and his dancing partner, and there was no attempt to perform a play (Colour Plate 9). Two variations of drumming are known to have existed, a restrained style and a more exuberant style. In another variation, a *dho-pat* (double-headed drum) was used.

The earliest type of drum dancing, which included songs and short sketches, was thought to have been first performed during the seventeenth century by a group accompanied by drummers playing on *bon-shay* (long drums). This version took its name from the 90-centimetre double-headed drum, which was hung from the player's neck. The group consisted of either one drummer, or a pair, accompanied by dancers and other musicians playing oboes, bamboo clappers, and cymbals. The picture in Colour Plate 10 is from a painting which shows King Theebaw being entertained, indicating that those taking part were court performers, appropriately and richly dressed. A rural group would have worn more casual clothes.

A later variation, which used even larger double-headed drums, came to be known as the *Shwebo-bongyi* (big drums of Shwebo), as it was seen only in the Shwebo district of Upper Burma. It is believed that this variation was first played during the reign of Alaungphaya (1752–60). As the group specialized in 'rain calling songs', it enjoyed popularity among rural folk, who claimed that if the seedlings were planted to the beat of the drums, a better harvest would be obtained. The Konbaung kings, whose ancestors were from Shwebo, maintained a troupe at the capital on a rota basis. Its duties included taking part in the annual ceremonial ploughing of the royal ricefields by the sovereign and his court, and other festive occasions.

When a troupe performed, people made offerings of flowers to the drums and to the local spirits. The drums, which could be as tall as a man, were too heavy to be carried and had to be supported either from a frame or a stand. A show, which could last for three nights, began about seven in the evening and ended about midnight. The performers taking part originally consisted of two drummers and a cymbal player, who stood in the middle and sang while he 'rubbed' the cymbals together, clashing them at the end of each stanza. All three postured and rotated, facing briefly, in turn, each side of the encircling audience.

With the addition of new characters, the cymbal player came to be known as the Drum Prince. He was accompanied by a youth dressed as the Drum Princess, and a clown. After singing traditional songs, they performed excerpts from plays, with each person assuming several roles. The little group did not receive money, but was fed and occasionally presented with clothing by the elders.

This form of drum dancing reached its peak in the late 1890s, and thereafter gradually declined. It was thought that this was partly due to some of the more gifted players leaving to join the thriving

42

theatrical troupes in the cities. Such simple shows were a major form of entertainment for the villagers in remote areas, where professional strolling players were reluctant to venture.

Dramatic Performances

In more accessible regions, rural folk had the opportunity of witnessing a *myai-waing*, or 'earth circling performance', as the action took place in an arena formed by the audience surrounding it. The word is the earliest known term for a dramatic performance by professionals accompanied by a full orchestra. Although presentation was still primitive by late nineteenth-century standards, it was the best that was available.

Shows were sometimes held during daylight hours, but despite poor lighting, night-time was more popular. Once the news had spread that a troupe had been hired (usually for three nights), crowds of people would appear in bullock carts, forming a huge ring, or *hle-waing*, around the audience (Plate 12).

In the centre of the 'stage', freshly cut branches were stuck into the ground to represent the forest which featured in most plays. Around this focal point were placed bamboos, with one end split and forced open to hold an oil-filled bowl with a wick. Above and behind the orchestra was a pole on which were hung masks of animals and demons for use during the performance (Plate 13). As the audience's powers of visualization were aided by the dialogue, the stark but illuminated area could assume any setting required by the play.

One authority has claimed that in the 'olden days' there were only four members in a troupe, consisting of the two leads, Gon-kaung (villain), and Kair-thu-shin (benevolent spirit) (U Min Naing, 1959). This would suggest that the scenario for all plays was predictable, with the couple being terrorized by the villain, and saved, at the end, by the spirit. But since he does not reveal his source, or date, it could be that this applied only to a particular group of players encountered by the original observer.

The segregated 'changing rooms' for the *myai-waing* players (with the men on the left, and the women on the right), was an

12. A *hle-waing* (cart circle) formed by the audience around the performance area. They camped here for the duration of the festival. From the *Illustrated London News*, April 1880.

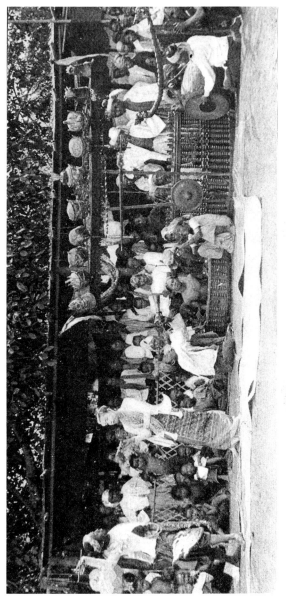

13. The principal dancers (*left*) from a *myai-waing* (earth circling) theatrical troupe, with the orchestra and masks on the right, late 1890s. From Max and Bertha Ferrars (1900).

45

area behind the musicians. There were no screens for privacy, so costume changes had to be made in the open. The costumes of the leading actor and actress, known as the Mintha (prince) and Minthamee (princess), were based on robes worn at court. During the play, both retained their rich silken clothes, even when required to portray a poor couple. Apart from using a mask, or by partly covering the body with a piece of cloth associated with a particular character—brown for a hermit or green for a demon—disguises were unknown.

In the performance area, the audience understood that if a king sat on a box it became a throne; the same box turned into a rustic retreat if used by a hermit. An undulating scarf symbolized a turbulent river, and if held in front of the hero and heroine, indicated that they were in difficulties in the water. At such times, the pair ran about with piteous cries for help, and often had the crowd panicked by the shrieks and noise from the orchestra.

Almost all plays included scenes in which the two leads were ill-treated, a situation which particularly appealed to the audience. Perhaps one's burden in real life was made easier to bear after witnessing another's even worse predicament. During such scenes, a *ngo-chin* (weeping song) was sung by actors and actresses alike, with dabbing of the eyes and beating of the chest to emphasize a word. The atmosphere of distress was further heightened by wailing sounds from the orchestra. Strong male characters were allowed to weep, for it was not considered unmanly.

It would seem that among the Burmese, songs in which the two leads lamented their fate were popular from an early period. The word *ngo-chin* first appeared in 1538, in the poem *Nay-mi-ngaye-khan-pyo* (*Nimi Jataka*) by Shin Aggathamadi, but doubtless such songs were being sung before that date. In a play, the audience's emotions were also manipulated by two other types of songs known as *lwan-chin* (longing songs) and *ngee-chin* (moaning songs). However, this does not mean that the entire performance was depressing. There were many other songs which were of a lively nature, and were sung during the first part of the show.

Prior to a performance, offerings were presented to the spirits, while the orchestra played a selection of tunes. An Ahpyodaw (maid of honour) then appeared and sang odes to the local and national spirits, calling for their blessing. She was followed by the Minthamee, who emerged from the right-hand side of the orchestra, and the Mintha, who was accompanied by the clowns, from the left. Possibly to show that the *myai-waing* troupe had its origins in drum dancing, the Mintha played on a double-headed drum suspended from his neck. This practice died out by the second half of the nineteenth century. A stately promenade around the central branch was then made by the couple and the clowns, singing and dancing.

When this scene ended, an audience with the king took place, at the end of which the couple, now dressed in their best costumes, reappeared with the clowns to perform the all-important duet. From about the 1860s, it became fashionable for a Mintha to carry a bow during this sequence. At the time, to gently place the curving, unstrung bow around his partner was considered daring (Plate 14).

Prior to the 1890s, the style in which the duet was danced was formal, with the couple keeping their distance. While the Minthamee performed, the Mintha had to stand still, with arms folded; it was said that if he moved, the audience made fun of him. This led to the male lead being called a *let-paik-Mintha* (Mintha with the folded arms)—a derisive term still used to describe someone who stands by idly, while another does all the work (Plate 15).

At about two o'clock in the morning, the play began. All the characters spoke in the stilted manner of the court; colloquial language was rarely used. The drama unfolded, and ended with the coming of the dawn light, with the good being rewarded, and the wicked punished.

From its humble beginnings among the mediums, religious pageants, and drum dancing, the theatre of the common people gradually emerged, and by the latter half of the nineteenth century had consolidated into well-organized touring companies.

47

14. A Mintha with a bow performing a duet in the old style, 1993.
(Courtesy of Sylvia Fraser-Lu)

15.   A Mintha and Minthamee with two clowns, late 1890s. From Max
      and Bertha Ferrars (1900).

Puppet Shows

Just as popular as the *myai-waing* were the *yoke-thay* (puppet shows).
Like the former, they began with a variety of song and dance
items, and ended with a dramatic play which lasted all night. The
dolls were cleverly manipulated and brought to life by vocalists
hidden behind a curtain. During the nineteenth century, the art of
puppetry found much favour among the common folk as well as
the court, and for a time was placed on a higher level than the live
theatre.

Chorus Dances

Another form of entertainment which invariably accompanied public celebrations was chorus dancing, performed by the children or young people of a community. The former sometimes enacted short sketches, and their perfect imitation of the professional actors often delighted and amused their elders (Colour Plate 11).

The word *yein* means 'to sway', and *yein ah-ka* (swaying dance) was the term used when a group moved in unison. The dancing took a variety of forms, and depended on the inventiveness of the choreographer. While the girls postured decorously (Colour Plate 12), the young men showed their skill with the martial stave dance, or played medium-sized double-headed drums. These drumming displays were so popular that theatrical companies began including them in their shows.

16.   A Shan *kinnaya* (mythical bird–man) dancer at a festival, *c.*1930. The costume is quite distinct from the Burmese version.

17. The author performing the dance of the *kinnaya* (mythical bird-man) at the Horniman Museum, London, 1966.

One of the oldest surviving chorus troupes, featuring a band of young men dressed as mythological beings called Zawgyi, is to be found at Phaunglin, in Central Burma. According to the opening words of their song, the Phaunglin Zaw Yein was first performed in 1783. The sixteen red-robed dancers, including a clown, are each armed with a short sword and a wand, and are led by two experienced 'masters' known as the Zaw Saya, who play on a gong and cymbals. The dancers taking part must be athletic as the movements, which have been preserved for generations, are energetic and the dancing lasts for two hours. A strict rule prescribes that only the youths of Phaunglin are eligible.

Like the Burmese, the numerous ethnic minorities in the country also celebrated their feast days with their own form of music, songs, and dances. Although group dancing was favoured by the majority of these tribes, among the Shan, solo dancers, performing either the dance of the *kinnaya* (Plates 16 and 17) or a dance with a pair of swords, were popular.

6

The Innovative Period of
Dance and Drama, 1886–1910

As we have seen, while the country was under a monarchy, entertainment was divided into two types, one for the palace, which was of a superior quality, and one for the people; the former was rarely accessible to the latter. But with the fall of the Konbaung Dynasty in 1885, commoners were able to experience for the first time the music and dances of the court.

When the British marched into Mandalay in 1885 and exiled the last of the Konbaung kings, the lives of thousands of courtiers were thrown into chaos. The next few years were traumatic for many, as new ways of earning a living had to be found.

Among the palace entertainers, the players who specialized in the *Ramayana* were the first to disperse, with some seeking employment with the *saobwa* (chiefs) in the Shan States, and others moving down to the prosperous regions of Lower Burma. As the palace restrictions no longer applied, many of the ex-court dancers, including the great theatrical luminaries who were by then middle-aged, were prepared to perform for anyone who would hire them. They brought with them the high standard of presentation which had once been exclusive to the palace theatre, and which the better class of theatrical companies eagerly adopted. However, by the mid-1890s, a new generation of Mintha and Minthamee began to replace the once famous former court dancers in popularity.

Tastes were changing in Mandalay, and the staid *Jataka* plays were being superseded by exciting new works from Rangoon. Over 300 plays are known to have been published between 1875 and 1915, either printed privately for guests attending a celebration, or for sale to the public. At first, the stories were original and competent, but soon, amateur playwrights began producing their own versions of popular plays and other stories. Although purists believed that the quality of composition deteriorated as a result, the public thought otherwise, and a number of editions were sold out soon after publication.

George Scott (Shway Yoe) (1882), commenting on the performing arts during the late 1870s, mentions a temporary theatre in Rangoon which charged admission fees, and concluded that it was 'an English idea'; previously, all shows were free. However, he does not say whether a stage and scenery were used by the players.

By about 1890, the rush to hold shows in theatres built in the Western style had gained momentum. At first, a few of the leading troupes experimented with only one backcloth, which was known as a *laphet-ye kar* (tea painting) as it resembled the label of a brand of tea popular at the time. These backdrops, which showed the turreted gateway of the Mandalay palace, could not be rolled up, and so remained fixed throughout the play, even when the plot called for the hero and heroine to journey through a forest, but soon the variety of props improved. In towns and cities, the simple 'earth circling' shows gave way to a stage with scenery, curtains, and modern lighting. Ideas for change were either acquired from Western magazines or from theatrical performances by visiting European companies.

In Mandalay, some of the older actors complained that it was difficult for them to ignore the old rule that only puppets be allowed the use of a stage. Those who made the break claimed that while performing, the booming of the *pat-ma* (huge double-headed drum) struck them in the chest with a violent force, and concluded that it was the spirit of the stage punishing them for their temerity. Soon many were grateful to be hired, and were prepared to perform anywhere.

In the late 1890s, the dancer Po Sein (1880–1952) became the first Mintha to charge admission to his theatre in Mandalay, which was a bamboo shed with a large area fenced in with matting (Plate 18). Some of the leading marionette and theatre troupes followed his example, but had to discontinue the practice as the audience stayed away.

With changes taking place in presentation, the poorer class of players could not afford the expensive trappings displayed by Po Sein and the other troupes, and had no option but to work

54

18. The old-style 'umbrella' structure (*left*) built over the performing area, and the back view of a 'modern' stage (below the central pavilion), Mandalay, *c*.1895.

the village circuits. In the remoter areas, the old 'earth circling' shows could still be seen until about 1915.

In the world of the theatre, the days of the prima donna were over, and the Mintha reigned supreme. Male leads with looks, voice, and dancing style, or the ability to assume any character required by the new plays from Lower Burma, were sought by theatrical companies, many of which came to be known by the name of their Mintha. As competition increased, so did the determination of the proprietors to secure a charismatic male lead. This sometimes involved bribery or subtle intimidation.

Scott informs us that two leads who were under contract to a better-class troupe in the 1870s were each paid between 800 and 1,000 rupees for the season, which began in October and ended the following May. Many, however, worked under stress, and constant travel, coupled with prolonged periods of sleepless nights, took their toll. Of the large number of Mintha and Minthamee listed in the numerous Burmese language articles on the theatre of the early 1900s, the working life of the majority did not last for more than five years.

Not all Mintha were handsome men. Po Kun, for example, the first husband of Ma Htway Lay, the Mandalay diva, had a dark, pock-marked skin, but he chose to specialize in plays such as *Kutha*, which featured an ugly hero. He was a brilliant actor, singer, and musician, and a perfect foil for his beautiful wife; the audience appreciated him.

Ekin Maung Gyi, on the other hand, was fair and good looking. Originally a farmer, he was trained by the former court puppeteer, Saya Pu, to play the Mintha vocalist in his marionette troupe. When Po Kun died, Ekin Maung Gyi married Ma Htway Lay, and the pair are said to have introduced many innovations in their shows. Another famous male lead was Sein Kho, a machinist, who had also been taught by Saya Pu, but later left the puppet stage for the theatre, where he enjoyed success.

Apart from capitalizing on the looks, voice, and dancing skills of the Mintha, the troupes contrived publicity in other ways. It could be in the unusual name of the male lead, or his strange obsessions on stage or in private life. Such stories were carefully circulated.

56

For example, during the three nights for which his troupe was hired, a Mintha called Sitthway would insist on including a play which had a monkey as the leading character, with the result that he was known as Myauk (monkey) Sitthway. Hlan (lance) Ko Sin became notorious for his villainous roles, in which he skilfully wielded a spear to kill off a character. His trick of seeming to pierce someone was so realistic that it horrified many among the audience. Kyar (tiger) Ko Thin invariably played the role of a hero who was changed into a tiger by bathing in a magical lake. Being an acrobat, his supple feline movements, performed in a tight-fitting tiger-skin costume, were popular.

Among the Minthamee, Yindaw Ma Lay, Sin Kho Ma Lay, and Ma Htway Lay, the three ex-divas of Mandalay, continued to hold the interest of the older generation until about the turn of the century. The first two ladies were already elderly, but they are said to have been well-preserved. Yindaw Ma Lay was occasionally hired by unkind people to dance with saucy young male leads who sang indelicate love songs to her (Dagon Khin Khin Lay, 1954). She died in her late seventies in near penury.

Fate was kinder to Ma Htway Lay. She was a brilliant actress, and when the monarchy ended, she turned professional and formed her own successful troupe. In the play *Ma Pada Maung Dartha*, in which she experienced great tribulations, losing her mind as a result, she would throw off her skirt and run about the stage in her flesh-coloured tights. The scene invariably caused an uproar, but attracted publicity. Ma Htway Lay also became famous for her 'flight dance'. When playing the role of the *kinnari* princess Dway Mai Naw, she would leap on to a large chest, and then appear to float down. Her pupil, Aung Bala (1882–1913), the female impersonator, took on the role when age made Ma Htway Lay incapable of performing this energetic dance (Cover Plate).

Some of the emerging Minthamee in Mandalay and elsewhere were sprightly girls who no longer believed in a court tradition. Many were not Burmese, and prefixed their name with that of the minority group to which they belonged; there was Pathi (Persian) Mya Nyunt and Ponna-ma (Manipuri) Ngwe Sein, and several from among the Arakanese, Karen, Shan, and Mon. One Burmese dancer deliberately called herself Bama-ma (Burmese) Thaing Chon.

Despite the changes, all theatrical companies continued to include the duet between the two leads, since it was unfailingly popular. The Mintha and Minthamee still danced separately, circling each other, as decency demanded that the space between the pair be fixed at 'the distance one hands a scarf or a fan'. But all this was to change when it was suggested to the Mintha Po Sein that he touch the Minthamee during the duet. He obliged by trying out a new sequence with Aung Bala, the female impersonator. It was claimed that the audience of the day, who were rather prudish about seeing a man and a woman touching in public, did not mind this intimacy between two men. Only when this form of dancing had become accepted, did Po Sein dare partner a female Minthamee. Soon, this innovation, which consisted only of the Mintha placing a flower in his lady's hair (an erotic connotation), and leading her by the hand during the promenade, was copied by other theatrical troupes.

Unlike the gentlemanly Po Sein, the Mintha Seinda, who had a reputation for his *risqué* love songs, unsettled some of the audience by dancing even closer to the Minthamee to the point of familiarity. He had a habit of chasing the 'protesting' lady around the stage, much to the delight of the young men in the audience. Such exhibitions were no doubt contrived, for in the entertainment world, which was becoming increasingly competitive, notoriety was one way of drawing a crowd.

Another 'crowd puller' employed by a theatrical proprietor was for a Mintha to appear as the leading lady, although it should be remembered that young men had been playing this role for several centuries in the drum dances of Shwebo, in Upper Burma.

The Mintha Sein Htaik was the first in this field, and had a fondness for the play *Maung Myitsaka*, in which the hero changes sex. In 1880, his troupe travelled to royal Mandalay and enjoyed enormous success. At the time, the bold style of presentation from British Burma must have been a revelation to the subjects of Theebaw. It was said that some men and women became enamoured of this fascinating creature, who could slip effortlessly into the role of either hero or heroine. Sein Htaik eventually became romantically involved with some female fans, as a result of which his life was threatened, and his troupe had to leave Mandalay in a hurry.

Sein Htaik was succeeded by the captivating Aung Bala, who had already been performing from his early teens and drew large crowds. In 1895, he found the ideal male lead in Po Sein, a partnership which lasted until 1898. As Aung Bala became even more successful, there was a constant change of Mintha, as relatively unknown and calculating young men used him to launch themselves into the world of the theatre.

Aung Bala occasionally appeared as a Mintha, but his fans preferred him in the role of the leading lady. At his death in 1913, the wild scenes of hysteria generated by hundreds of his female fans, many rolling on the ground, caused a sensation throughout the country. A dance style known as the Aung Bala still exists.

Conversely, some women took to appearing as the male lead, but were derided by the audience. Yet, at the time, the most popular act in variety shows preceding a play consisted of a Minthamee dressed as a Mintha, and playing a heavy *ozi* drum (Plate 19).

In the theatre, the sequence in which each item appeared followed the traditional order for about a decade after 1885, but thereafter many new dance forms replaced the established ones. Only one item, the dance of the Ahpyodaw (maid of honour) was retained, as her duty consisted of propitiating the spirits to ensure that there were no mishaps during the performance (Plate 20).

The role was originally danced by an experienced, middle-aged lady, and was an amalgam of the movements used by mediums connected with the thirty-seven national spirits. During the second and third nights, this was changed to the 'twelve styles' associated with an alchemist, demon, elephant, horse, hermit, king, minister, monkey, prince, princess (Colour Plate 13), spirit medium, and tiger—dance movements borrowed from the puppet theatre. However, by the early 1900s, alterations had been made and only six of the original character dances had survived.

On the first night, the programme began with the Ahpyodaw coming on to the stage with the mincing walk of a puppet, to sing and dance an invocation to the spirits. However, her solemn

19.   The *ah-nyeint* Minthamee Aye Sein dressed as a Mintha and performing the *Ozi* dance, *c.*1910.

20. An Ahpyodaw (maid of honour) wearing the headband of a spirit medium, with offerings to the right, 1993. (Courtesy of Sylvia Fraser-Lu)

demeanour changed as soon as the song ended, and the dancing became livelier, with good-natured banter between her and the orchestra, the latter trying their best to exhaust her by playing faster. The item lasted for about thirty minutes, and was followed by variety acts, short sketches, and finally a dramatic performance.

Perhaps because of the large number of shows which were constantly being held, the audience became sated, and in the late 1890s it became fashionable to hire an orchestra simply to hear it play. These performances were called *balar-saing*, meaning that they were not accompanied by either dancers or singers. As the trend increased, there was fierce competition and some of the musicians used gimmicks to attract custom.

One orchestra leader called Sagaing Saya Nyo used to play the drum-circle wearing a demon mask, and with peacock feathers attached to his wrists, signifying that he had 'flying fingers' which could produce the most melodious of sounds. Not to be outdone, Saya Seint (1872–1916), the leading musician of the period, and a former member of the court orchestra, played a similar instrument while balancing a cup of water on his head, not an easy task as the player had to twist and turn to reach the numerous drums with which he was surrounded.

The theatrical profession did not realize it at the time, but a rival was about to emerge and compete with them for the attention of the public. These small troupes were composed of young female dancers, and had their origins at court.

Palace regulations were so ingrained that many of the surviving *nan-dwin-ah-nyeint* (the king's female entertainers) could not bring themselves to perform for mere commoners. However, such inhibitions did not hamper the new and ambitious younger dancers of Mandalay. They persuaded the more talented of these ex-court ladies to instruct them, with the result that the city witnessed the rebirth of the *ah-nyeint* troupe in the early 1890s. Their patrons were the newly rich and some of the remaining members of the royal family. As this form of entertainment became popular, a clown was added, and the number of musical instruments increased.

At first, the elegant style of the ex-court dancers was faithfully followed, but from about the mid-1890s, changes began to take place. The traditional instruments, such as the crocodile harp, the curved harp, and the reed pipe, were considered old-fashioned and were replaced by a small orchestra. While one troupe specialized in the *htaing-so* (seated singing), another performed the *ah-ka* (dance) only; some troupes combined both.

The costume of these young ladies consisted of an embroidered bodice and an open-fronted, tight-fitting, long-sleeved jacket. From the waist, two crescent shapes jutted out like wings, sweeping back behind the dancer. Although the silk skirt was of native manufacture, the elaborate *ah-cheik*, or wavy-line patterns of the nineteenth century, were no longer in vogue. According to Scott (1882), by the early 1880s, this type of design was being dismissed as 'provincial' by the young of Lower Burma. Tiny checks, stripes, and vertical abstract patterns had become fashionable.

In the world of the theatre, the Mintha had replaced the Minthamee in importance, and as some of the leading ladies did not find this to their liking, they decided to form their own all-female dance troupes. Such artistes were to change this once refined entertainment, turning it into something which became unrecognizable from the earlier courtly performances.

The idea of an all-female dance troupe was also taken up in Lower Burma, and Saya Phyu (d. 1918), a harpist, is credited with being the first to have organized a show in Rangoon during the 1890s. He claimed that a female student of his could not refrain from making dance movements during her harp lessons, and unwittingly invented the characteristic *ah-nyeint* dance of Rangoon. No information is available as to how the student managed to combine both activities, or in which way the dance differed from the original style. Perhaps the Rangoon version was considered 'modern', while the Mandalay style was more sedate.

By about 1910, Kemmindine, in Rangoon, had become renowned for its large community of entertainers, among whom were the *ah-nyeint* troupes. One of the most successful dancers of this period was the beautiful Sein Chit, who was also in great demand as a model for European photographers; her picture often appeared on postcards (Plate 21). It was said that at the beginning of her career as a dancer, she had to be literally pushed on to the

21. Sein Chit (*standing*), one of the leading *ah-nyeint* Minthamee, with her sister, *c.*1910. They are not wearing their stage costume.

performing area as she suffered from severe stage fright.

Photographs from the period show that none of the dancers wore the fixed, artificial smile which has become the norm since the 1950s. No matter what her reputation, it was not considered proper for the Minthamee to smile at strange men. Some of the jokes shouted by the clowns brought roars of laughter, but they were often coarse; yet the dancer's face had to remain mask-like.

Although the clown had become indispensable, he occupied an inferior position to the Minthamee. He sometimes cracked jokes at her expense, which she pretended not to hear or, if she did, smacked him with her fan. Many clowns were gifted songwriters and playwrights. They were also good actors and dancers, but took care not to outshine the star of the show.

Spurred on by competition, these all-female dancing troupes began to evolve rapidly. Not content with merely singing and dancing, a proprietor named San Nyunt decided to include a short play in his shows. This was quickly copied by rival troupes, who sometimes performed in the street (Colour Plate 14). His protégée, Ma Thein May, became the first *ah-nyeint* Minthamee to play the part of a Mintha (Colour Plate 15).

7

Dance and the Theatre, 1911–1993

THE preference for holding performances on a stage became so established that other forms of entertainment, such as group dances, musical ensembles, one-man shows, and even religious pageants, adopted the idea. In the Burmese quarters of Rangoon in the early 1900s, the organizers of *nebhatkhin* replaced the traditional caravan of carts with small platforms built along a processional way. Each of these bamboo structures was decorated to look like a stage set, and contained scenes from the birth stories of Buddha. In some, minor actors and actresses were hired to portray the principal characters.

By 1911, the number of theatrical companies had increased even further, with many a proprietor becoming wealthy. To their credit, some used their profits to produce better plays. Presentation, too, began to improve, as the stage was now illuminated by the latest equipment from the West.

The star who now outshone all others in the theatrical firmament was the Mintha Po Sein. He changed the traditional sequence of a show by adding more variety items, including young chorus dancers (Plate 22). Po Sein's staging of the chilling play *Hti Lat Po U* was such a success that Ahuja, the leading postcard company in Rangoon, took the unusual step of printing a card with one of the gory scenes in which the villain removes the foetus from his lover's womb to use in a magical rite (Plate 23). It is known that in another play, *Kutha*, he sang forty songs; this record has not been matched. While many a Mintha of his generation enjoyed fame briefly, Po Sein was still dancing at the age of seventy-two, and literally danced himself to death during a performance in 1952.

In a bid to present novel themes, the shows staged by the better-class companies consisted of exotically dressed chorus girls who performed with an assortment of musical instruments. Celebrated *ah-nyeint* personalities, too, were hired to take part. As such variety items had been introduced by the remarkable Po Sein, they came

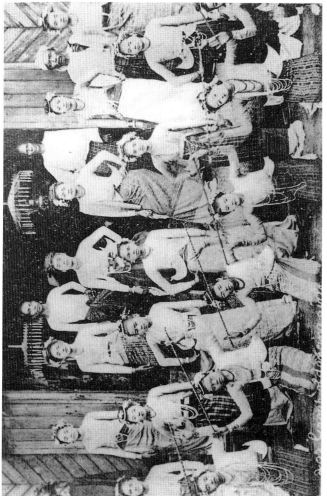

22. A professional *yein* troupe of chorus girls, with the Mintha (*centre*) and the leading ladies at the back, c.1915.

23. Po Sein's macabre play *Hti Lat Po U* was so popular that a postcard was issued by Ahuja of Rangoon. Postmark dated 1903.

to be known as a Po Sein Pwe (Po Sein Show), irrespective of the company's name.

Perhaps because of the surplus of female dancers, many of the leading companies began increasing the number of Minthamee to partner their solitary Mintha (Plate 24). This resulted in scenes described as *lin-lu-pwe* (husband grabbing shows). Despite its lurid claim, an item of this nature consisted merely of the numerous Minthamee showing off their dance expertise to attract the attention of the male lead.

Among the Mintha of this period, one who gripped the public imagination was an English youth called John Hammond. He had fallen in love with a Burmese dancing girl, and had joined her troupe at the age of fifteen. Being adaptable, he trained to take on the role of the Mintha, with the stage name of Shwe Daung (Golden Peacock)—a remarkable feat! Hammond was instantly ostracized by the British community for having turned so blatantly 'native', but was received with open arms by the Burmese. They nicknamed him In-ga-lan Sein (English Diamond).

24. A Mintha dancing with a group of Minthamee, 1993. (Courtesy of
Sylvia Fraser-Lu)

Despite the success of the theatre, it was the all-female dancing
troupes which were in demand. These shows were now miniature
copies of the theatre, and were also cheaper to hire. The proprietors
ranged from merchants to civil servants, such as Sir James Mg Gyi,
who in 1922 set up a group featuring some of the most beautiful
dancers. But his young ladies were only to be seen at official
functions and garden parties.

In the all-female dance shows, the Minthamee appeared in
reverse order of seniority, the youngest first; each item was allowed
about an hour. The dancer stepped on to the stage from behind the
orchestra and, ignoring the audience, sat with her back to them.
The two clowns would then recite glowing verses about her
dazzling beauty, and 'persuade' her to perform. She would then
turn around in a condescending manner and sing in a shrill voice,
fashionable at the time. The style of singing was a medley of
classical, 'updated' classical, and modern songs. When the song
ended, she danced, slowly at first, and then with increasingly faster

movements, leaping and twisting, her rubber-like arms and hands becoming a blur under the lights. The music usually stopped with a sudden crash, and she would momentarily freeze in the final position. She sometimes bowed to the audience, or simply turned her back and fanned herself vigorously.

When the British Empire Exhibition opened at Wembley, London, in 1924, a troupe of Burmese dancers appeared, but received a mixed reception; it would seem that the performances were a trifle too strident and exotic for the British taste.

It is from this period that the professional *ah-nyeint* Minthamee began adopting a haughty manner, an attitude which could still be seen among performers until the early 1960s. The reason is not known. Perhaps this was a defensive ploy, for the girls knew only too well that they were fair game for any character assassins from rival companies who were in the crowd.

During the 1930s, the demeanour of many a Minthamee was to undergo an additional change. She now flirted with her audience, singing songs which came to be known as *ye-sar-hmaw* (longing for a lover), with coy, simpering glances. Yet, at the end of each item, she assumed her original icy aloofness and, no doubt, titillated many of her male fans with these swift behavioural changes. Her dance movements were now even less graceful, and quite alien to the original *ah-nyeint* dance forms of the court, which were elegant and stately displays.

Photographs of Minthamee from the period show unsmiling, dead-white faces, with thinly pencilled eyebrows and rose-bud mouths, reminiscent of the Hollywood beauties who were to be seen in the local cinemas. Their hair, carefully coiled into a huge cylindrical shape, was copiously padded out with false hairpieces, and wreathed in flowers and ornaments. Among the dancers, the silk skirts of native manufacture were now considered dated. In fashion were satin and other foreign materials, embroidered with sequins and brilliants. The designs were usually of exotic birds, fussy bows, and huge floral patterns, which were not typically Burmese (Plate 25).

In the theatre, rivalry between companies also led to some startling costume innovations. The Mintha Sein Gadon became

25. The *ah-nyeint* dancer from 1870, the 1930s, and 1993.

71

one of the first dancers to have small electric light bulbs (Christmas tree decorations) formed into a *salwe* (badge of office), which was worn in the shape of an 'X' across the chest; the lights flashed as he danced. Other Mintha had their entire costume covered in these tiny bulbs—a hazardous indulgence as the movements were often vigorous despite the trailing wires.

Many of the male leads, such as the debonair Sabair (Jasmine) Tin, a brilliant dancer, are remembered not for their contributions to the performing arts, but for the scandals left in their wake; he ran off with the senior wife of the Chief of Hsipaw, in the Shan States (Plate 26).

Some of the traditionalists among the better class of professionals became concerned at the changes taking place, and at the 'updating' of many of the classical songs by 'progressive' songwriters, and in 1931 decided to establish the Mahagita College. As recording companies, such as Columbia, were issuing Burmese plays and modern songs, members of the college were able to arrange for their authentic versions to be accepted; the records are said to have enjoyed a certain degree of success.

Away from the big towns and cities, life went on as usual for the country folk. Some had never ventured outside their village boundaries, and were unaware of the marvels that were being presented by the modern theatrical companies. Many made their own entertainment, and there were always the young men and girls of the village who could be relied on to perform the popular chorus dances.

During the Second World War, almost all the theatrical companies were forced to break up, as most of their members returned to their villages in the belief that they would be safe there. When the Japanese Army occupied the country, it was not considered prudent to parade the nation's dancing maidens before them. Occasionally, the elderly Po Sein performed for the Japanese generals, but full-scale shows were absent for some time. At Buddhist festivals, which were still being observed, amateur groups would put on an all-male display. When the war ended in 1945, Burma swarmed with Allied troops. Within weeks, refugees, including those from the entertainment industry, returned to the

26. The Mintha Sabair Tin on the steps of the Shan palace at Hsipaw,
     c.1930s. The traditionally woven *pasoe* has been replaced by one of
     appliqué, sequins, and brilliants.

devastated towns and cities. After the years of hardship, costumes and props were hurriedly put together for the celebratory shows.

Although Burma gained her independence from Britain in 1948, life was disrupted by insurgency, which made travel nearly impossible. However, the theatrical companies and the puppet troupes regrouped, and when opportunity permitted they were in a better position to hold a performance. Nevertheless, it was not until the early 1950s that a precarious stability returned.

One of the rising Mintha of this period was Shweman Tin Maung, who had already begun to make a name for himself in the late 1930s. After the war, he continued to enjoy success, and was highly thought of, by purists and audiences alike, for his revival of the traditional styles. There were also other Mintha, such as Sein Aung Min and Kenneth Sein. The latter was the son of Po Sein, who, despite his advanced years, still made brief appearances.

The people were becoming aware of their culture and heritage, and in 1953 a committee was formed at the Cultural Institute in Rangoon to classify the various dances from the nineteenth century. It was soon discovered that sometimes the name had survived, but the dance itself had been altered. Fortunately, there were still dancers who could tell the difference, and with their help, adjustments were made. State Schools for the Fine Arts were opened in Rangoon and Mandalay in 1953.

Training for students of dance begins with an exercise called *gabyar-lut*, which consists of twenty unrelated movements. However, performed to drum music, the movements flow smoothly from one to the other, and are claimed to be the basic steps from which other variations can be created.

In the training sequence, the male student begins with hands on hips, bending sideways, first to the left, and then to the right. While one foot takes the weight of the body, the other touches the floor lightly with the heel. These leg movements alternate throughout the entire dance; both feet are never allowed to be placed flat on the ground. Although it is considered proper for men to dance with the knees bent and held open, such an indelicate posture is never adopted by a lady.

74

The dance training for the female students consists of imitating the movements performed by puppets, and learning how to move in the confining sack-like skirt without falling over. Training dances for both male and female students end in the puppet pose known as 'when the strings are cut', in which the dancers fall to the floor in an effortless manner, and remain frozen for a short while. Since it was first introduced nearly forty years ago, many variations have been added to the *gabyar-lut*. It is still used by professionals who have refined and rearranged some of the movements to their personal taste.

The 1950s were a creative period. As if to make up for time lost during the war years, the entertainment industry experimented with new ideas. Modern melodrama, called *pya-zat*, became popular, and was shown together with the variety acts during the first half of an all-night performance.

In Rangoon, although Burmese and foreign films were usually playing to full houses, and competing successfully with the traditional forms of entertainment, some cinemas were turned into theatres to satisfy public demand for the *pya-zat*, which rarely dealt with historical or Buddhist stories. These modern plays, in contemporary costumes, drew vast audiences as they featured popular and glamorous film stars of the day. Some of the more famous Mintha, such as Sein Aung Min, also made films of their stage shows, but these were not well received.

Among the *ah-nyeint* troupes of the early 1960s, the stage was well equipped, and ultra-violet lighting made the costumes glow. The old graceful style of dancing, too, was making a comeback. Some companies engaged as many as six dancers, with the lead Minthamee making a grand entrance for her part of the show; this was followed by a play. While some of the lesser known troupes finished their performances at midnight, a few of the bigger names continued until dawn.

In the world of the theatre, Shweman Tin Maung was still the premier star, with Sein Aung Min and Kenneth Sein ranked next. For some, Kenneth Sein was considered too modern; he surprised many audiences by breaking into a tap-dancing routine while performing a traditional Burmese dance. Purists pointed out that his hybrid tastes manifested themselves even in his costume, with its curious 1920s European-style cape. Sadly, the 1960s were to close with the death of Shweman Tin Maung, who died while performing the ever popular dance duet.

In the 1970s, many a critical article appeared in the leading newspapers and magazines about the haphazard way in which shows were being presented, although these criticisms had little or no effect on the culprits. Chin Aung (1985), for one, said that theatrical shows were hurriedly put together to make a 'quick killing'. He noted that the acting was appalling, and that the standard of dancing had deteriorated. Characters such as a king and his courtiers, or mythological beings, could no longer use the accepted language of the traditional theatre. He pointed out that story-lines were so far-fetched and confused that many in the audience came away irritated; having spent a sleepless night on a bamboo mat could not have helped either.

For the young hopefuls in the entertainment profession, there are no theatrical agencies. Recruitment is by word of mouth, or application direct to a company. Needless to say, there are numerous moral dangers for the naïve. Since the introduction of video during the 1980s, artistes from the low-paid theatrical profession are said to have joined the ranks of this thriving industry. Although scripts with a moral message and those which activate patriotic feelings are said to be encouraged by the government, scenes of violence are on the increase—a theme which is said to be also favoured in the theatre. Many troupes now employ two orchestras, a traditional and a modern one, the latter composed of the latest Western-style instruments—usually from Japan.

The Burmese movie industry, which began in 1918, was partly responsible for the demise of some of the traditional forms of entertainment, such as the now almost defunct puppet shows, but in 1995 it, too, is in danger from the influx of foreign videos, and those produced by local companies. It costs less to film on video tape, and the remuneration is considerable. A disturbing new trend at pagoda festivals is the appearance of booths showing blue videos, and other such-like entertainment.

While dance and drama performances by professionals have undergone changes, one art form—the perennial *Ramayana*—has remained the same (Plate 27). Some recent accounts by European writers have claimed that the epic is rarely seen these days. On the contrary, in 1981 thirteen amateur companies in Lower Burma were listed as holding annual performances.

In Upper Burma, three companies are known among the Manipuri communities of Amarapura, Mandalay, and Sagaing. These groups were formed in the nineteenth century and give perform-ances in Manipuri and Burmese. In their shrine in Mandalay, the masks of the principal characters from the *Ramayana* are preserved; the attendants here double as astrologers. The descendants of the court dancers of Ayutthaya also have a shrine in the city, where the masks are on display (Plate 28). Many of the universities and colleges encourage their students to stage excerpts from this much loved play.

Although the masks cannot be compared to the superb *khon* examples from Thailand, it should be noted that while the latter are produced by trained mask-makers, the Burmese versions are the efforts of enthusiastic amateurs; only one professional mask-maker is known in Rangoon (Colour Plate 16). The ceremony of *puja* (worship) is performed each year for the masks, at the beginning and end of the Buddhist lent, when *than-sin-pan* (*Bulbophyllum* sp.) (orchids) are offered.

According to Khin Maung Htay (1982), Indonesia hosted a seminar in 1971 on the influence of the *Ramayana* in South-East Asia, together with dance displays from the relevant countries. Since then, there has been a revival, with paintings, masks, and dolls being made for sale. Recent communications received by the author indicate that the annual shows are still held, but that these are now condensed versions, and last from three to seven nights, as opposed to the original forty-five. Despite pressures for change, the actors of the *Ramayana* have safeguarded the old gestures handed down to them by the court dancers of Ayutthaya.

For those who care about the survival of the traditional performing arts, it is a relief to know that while the standards of the commercially managed shows have deteriorated, those organized

27. A performance of the *Ramayana*, c.1959. Rama is being persuaded by Sita to catch the golden deer. Ministry of Union Culture, Rangoon.

28. A shrine for the masks from the *Ramayana*, Mandalay, in use by the descendants of the court dancers of Ayutthaya, 1994. Newly painted masks represent the Hermit, Rama, Sita, and Lakshmana. (Courtesy of Shwebo Mi Mi Gyi)

by amateurs have managed to maintain the old traditions. In the big cities, classical dance classes are popular. According to recent newspaper accounts, in the countryside, too, folk-dances are being revived. Although the ancient religious pageant of *nebhatkhin* almost vanished in the 1930s, there was an impressive revival in Rangoon in the 1950s.

Another variation of this pageant is still preserved at Monywa, in Upper Burma. There, the displays are of two types: the *win-khin*, where historical incidents are depicted, and the *day-wa-khin*, which is referred to as a parade of benevolent Buddhist spirits. A small group of musicians accompany the procession, which either proceeds on foot or on decorated lorries.

The State Schools for the Fine Arts in Mandalay and Rangoon still teach dancing and drama, and their best students can be seen at tourist centres. State-sponsored troupes also go on tour and are generating new interest among the young. Old dance styles, based on wall-paintings, are being re-created, and long-forgotten plays from the nineteenth century are occasionally staged at the National Theatre in Rangoon.

In September 1993, the military government organized competitions for seven days in Rangoon for singers of classical songs, musicians playing traditional instruments, and dancers performing in the old court style. Considering that the participants were amateurs, the singing and music were reportedly of the highest quality, and the dances were competently executed. However, one should not be too complacent. Now that the Bamboo Curtain has finally lifted, and access is easy, young Burmese, who are the future patrons of the arts, are increasingly being seduced by Western culture, in particular, rock music. As a lover of all that is uniquely Burmese, it is the author's hope that the gilded gong-circle will not be replaced by the electronic synthesizer.

8

Burma's Alternative Theatre

TOURISTS visiting Burma may come across what they assume to be theatrical shows taking place in the streets, only to learn that they are, in fact, witnessing propitiatory ceremonies to the *nat* (spirits) of the country. The rituals include enactment of scenes from the stories of the thirty-seven national spirits, many of which had their lives terminated in an unpleasant way.

Like particular characters from an epic, each entity has a distinctive personality, mannerisms, and costume. Almost all their pictorial representations carry swords and palm-leaf fans, the symbolism being that they could be utterly ruthless, and cut one down in their anger, or, if propitiated, bring cooling peace with their fan.

The rich diversity of their life stories made a natural subject for plays, which were often performed in the live theatre and on the marionette stage. Mediums who organize the spirit shows are aware of the power of dramatic presentation, and tend to select the more tragic or blood-curdling tales. A combination of dance, music, murder, and the supernatural never fails to hold the interest of the public, who are encouraged to make a substantial donation.

Early man, no doubt, thought it sensible to appease the unseen forces. In historical times, indigenous spirits, together with the gods of Buddhism and Hinduism, were worshipped by the Pyu, the Mon, and later by the Burmese. The most ancient among the numerous spirits which still have a firm hold on the nation's psyche are Pyu in origin.

Almost all these beings were historical figures who died tragically. Over the centuries, their memories have been kept alive by the medium fraternity. Members of this ancient profession, whose livelihood depended on the public, have preyed on the susceptible minds of the people. They claim that the spirits are unpredictable, and if offended are liable to take revenge unless propitiated through them.

During ceremonies called *nat-pwe* (spirit show), animals were once slaughtered, and the intoxicated mediums performed in wild abandon. In time, because of protests from the Buddhist clergy and the civil authorities, the dancing became more controlled, and appropriate gestures, together with a ritual song for each spirit, evolved.

It would appear that no stigma was attached to the profession, and people from all walks of life were drawn to it. The kings Minhkaung (r. 1401–22) and Mohnyinthado (r. 1427–40) both spent their youth as spirit-dancers. A view held by some scholars is that when mediums decided to become strolling players, they incorporated the movements used in their previous profession into their dance routines (Maung Htin Aung, 1937; U Min Naing, 1959).

In 1805, spirit worship came under the scrutiny of the crown, and a commission was set up to investigate the mediums and their rituals. On the committee were Myawaddy Wungyi U Sa, the playwright, and an official known as the Nat-htein (Guardian of the Spirits) whose department organized such ceremonies at court. Hundreds of mediums were summoned to the capital, and a thorough investigation made. It was decreed that the costume, song, and ritual movements for each spirit be followed correctly. U Sa also rewrote the songs of the thirty-seven spirits; these are autobiographical in nature, and are sung with dramatic action. The results of the commission were later collated and published in the *Mahagita Maydane Kyam* (1881).

In 1812, a report submitted by the Lord of Popa, the premier cult centre on the summit of an extinct volcano known as Popa-taung (flower mountain), said that the musical instruments for the Mahagiri spirit consisted of one small and seven large red drums, a rattle, a silver oboe, a trumpet, and cymbals. But by the late 1860s, in the *nat* 'palace' at Taungbyon, the second most important cult centre and one dedicated to the two Shwephyin Nyinaung spirits, a full orchestra was in use (Colour Plate 17). Many of the male and female mediums who lived in the region were obliged to attend the annual festival as the role was hereditary (Plate 29). These obligations also extended to the musicians who played 'spirit music',

29.   A male trance-dancer at Taungbyon, the spirit cult centre near
       Mandalay, in the late 1950s.

and in many cases were undertaken through fear of punishment
from these entities.

The medium was originally called *nat-win-the* (one whom the
spirit enters), but came to be known as *nat-kadaw* (spouse of the
spirit) in the nineteenth century. A medium told fortunes and of-
ficiated at private functions and at the annual festivals at cult centres
throughout the country. When performing her duties, the instructions listed in the *Mahagita Maydane Kyam* were strictly followed, as
improvization was once held to be extremely dangerous.

The list included the type of dress to be worn when propitiating
a particular *nat*. For example, a medium impersonating the spirit of
a king could not wear a robe cut in the royal style, but could only
appear in a white, spangled dress with voluminous sleeves, and a
turban wrapped in the shape of a crown. Appropriate attributes of

the deity also had to be carried, together with sprigs of the auspicious *tha-byai* (*Eugenia grandis*), a type of myrtle.

A ritual began with the medium bowing to the image of the spirit. This was followed by chanting of its song, which listed the main events in its life, and finally, by dancing. At this stage, possession had not yet taken place, for the medium danced in a conscious state to entertain the spirit. Later, possession began with the medium trembling; and the entity then spoke through her. Sometimes, there was further dancing; it was believed that it was the spirit amusing itself.

During possession, and depending on the personality of any one of the thirty-seven spirits, the medium either became wild and rowdy, as the alcoholic Min Kyawzwa, or coy and playful, if possessed by the Little Lady Flute. The ritual reached its climax with the dancer going into convulsions, a sign that the spirit was about to leave. She was then sprinkled with water from the altar and left to recover.

When the unsophisticated mind was confined by fear and an unquestioning belief in tradition, the dance forms were rigorously preserved. Once that fear was erased during this century, innovations emerged, and the mediums had no one to please but themselves.

Nowadays a spirit show takes place in a temporary hall, with an altar and an orchestra. The central arena is reserved for the mediums, who are surrounded by the devotees and onlookers; the arrangement is remarkably like that of the now defunct *myai-waing* (earth circling performances). Originally, only 'spirit music' was played, but since the 1930s many of the tunes have become mixed, and now songs and music from the theatre are included. The costume of the medium, too, has become hardly distinguishable from those seen in films and theatrical productions.

Modern-day mediums are usually female, and come from all classes, but with uneducated women predominating. Although men are known, those who have turned professional since the 1950s are mainly transvestites—a post-war phenomenon (Plate 30). The reason appears to be twofold. As the 'spouse of the spirit', they are entitled to flaunt their femininity in appropriate clothes. Also,

30. A transsexual trance-dancer in modern dress, feigning possession by a *nat* (spirit). The orchestra with an effeminate singer is in the background, Monywa, Upper Burma, 1987.

as many of the people are superstitious by nature, they are less likely to make fun of an effeminate man who has 'access' to a malevolent *nat*. Large numbers of transvestite dancers have also infiltrated the theatre, and have become established members of many a company.

In the past, it was the strolling players who imitated the movements of the mediums, but now, it is the latter who copy the dances performed in the theatre. Almost all their original ritual gestures have been abandoned. The few traditional ones which remain are recognizable in the curious swaying of the upper part of the body, with the arms forming ribbon-like movements around the trunk.

Mediums claim that they can induce possession by bowing to an image. However, many are adept at acting, and can convincingly fake a trance. In genuine cases of possession, the symptoms include glazed eyes and violent movements. Members of the public sometimes become 'possessed', and dance in a grotesque manner; it is understood by the onlookers that during such moments individuals are not responsible for their actions. Once the frenzy has passed, the participant claims a sense of immense relief. Money is then demanded by the organizers for this privileged feeling of well-being.

Until 1959, three types of 'trance-dancing' were believed to have existed in the Lower, Central, and Upper regions of the country. These variations were among the Burmese only, and since the 1980s have become fused due to lack of control from a central authority. The Arakanese, Chin, Kachin, Mon, and Shan also have their spirits, which are propitiated in their own way with dancing, but little research has been done in these areas.

Recent reports from Burma indicate that at the spirit shows, transvestites now predominate; they sing, dance, and perform short sketches. The imbibing of alcohol, which until the 1960s was viewed with horror, is unrestricted, as it is handed around by the inebriated mediums, and drunk as an offering. Amidst the raucous vulgarity, shady business deals are transacted. As a result, the ceremonies have lost their mystique, and are being taken less seriously by many. They are accepted as pure theatre and, at some of the cult centres, as an excuse for an orgiastic feast.

A plaintive *nat* song for the spirit of the ten-year-old Prince Nawratha, who was put into a velvet sack and ceremonially drowned at Ah Wa by his uncle, Shwenankyawshin (r. 1502–27), says that it longs to sleep. But it is doubtful whether the mediums will permit it while there is a demand for this lucrative industry.

Select Bibliography

Ba Han, 'Evolution of Burmese Dramatic Performances and Festive Occasions', *Journal of the Burma Research Society*, Vol. XLIX, No. 1, Rangoon, June 1966.

Chin Aung, 'Pwe Kyi Mi Par Thee Khin Byar' [I Have Seen a Play], *Thaung Pyaung Htwai Lar*, Rangoon, April 1985.

Cox, Hiram, *Journal of a Residence in the Burmhan Empire, and more particularly at the Court of Amarapoorah*, John Warren, London, 1821.

Crawfurd, J., *Journal of an Embassy from the Governor-General of India to the Court of Ava*, London, 1829.

Dagon Khin Khin Lay, 'Mya Galay hnin Theingi' [Queen Mya Galay and the Play Theingi], *Ngwetaryi*, Rangoon, 1950s.

———, 'Myanmar Zat Thabin' [Burmese Theatre], *Myawaddy*, Rangoon, 1954.

Dagon Nat Shin, 'Myanmar Yinkyaihmu Thukhuma Thabin' [Burmese Theatre], *Yinkyaihmu*, Rangoon, 1950s.

Dalrymple, A., *Oriental Repertory*, William Ballantine, London, 1808.

Ferrars, Max and Ferrars, Bertha, *Burma*, Sampson Low, Marston and Co., London, 1900.

Fytche, Albert, *Burma Past and Present*, Kegan Paul, London, 1878.

Grant Brown, R., *Burma As I Saw It (1889–1917)*, Methuen and Co., London, 1926.

Hall, D. G. E. (ed.), *Michael Symes: Journal of His Second Embassy to the Court of Ava in 1802*, George Allen and Unwin Ltd., London, 1955.

Herbert, Patricia M., *The Life of the Buddha*, British Library, London, 1993.

Hla Pe, *Komara Pya Zat: An Example of Popular Drama in the XIX Century by U Pok Ni*, Vol. I, Luzac, London, 1952.

Hman-nan Maha Yazawindawgyi [Glass Palace Chronicle], 3 vols., Pyigyimantaing Pitika Press, Rangoon, 1967.

Htin Aung, Maung, *Burmese Drama: A Study, with Translation, of Burmese Plays*, Oxford University Press, Calcutta, 1937.

Khin Maung Htay, 'Yama Yarpyi Pwe Daw ko Kyo So Par Thee' [Welcome to the Rama Centenary], *Yadanamun*, Rangoon, January 1982.

Khin Min, Maung, 'Shin Maha Ratthasara e Zatkaung Ahphwair'

[The Creation of Characters by Shin Maha Ratthasara], *Ngwetaryi*, Rangoon, 1976.

Laurie, W. F. B., *Our Burmese Wars*, Allen, London, 1880.

Mahagita [Book of Songs], Cultural Institute, Rangoon, 1954.

Mahagita Maydane Kyam [Book of Odes and *Nat* Songs], U Yauk, Thayae Khittaya (Prome), 1881.

Man-shu-chiao-chu, also known as *The Man Shu* [Book of the Southern Barbarians], translated by G. E. Luce, Cornell University, Ithaca, 1961.

Maung Maung Tin, U, 'Pwe Kyi Saung Ahkyaung' [About the Royal Theatre], Shumawa, Rangoon, 1950s.

Min Naing, U, *Pyidaungsu Akha Padaythar* [Dances of the Union of Burma], Ministry of Union Culture, Rangoon, 1959.

Myanmar Swairson Kyam (*Encyclopedia Birmanica*), 15 vols., Burma Translation Society, Rangoon, 1954–76.

Ono Toru, *The Burmese Versions of the Rama Story and Their Peculiarities*, Osaka University of Foreign Studies, Osaka, 1993.

Rodrigue, Yves, *Nat Pwe: Burma's Supernatural Sub-Culture*, Kiscadale Publications, Gartmore, 1992.

Sangermano, Vincentius, *The Burmese Empire a Hundred Years Ago*, Archibald Constable & Co., London, 1893.

Shway Yoe (Sir George Scott), *The Burman, His Life and Notions*, Macmillan and Co., London, 1882; reprinted Kiscadale Publications, Edinburgh, 1989.

Singer, Noel F., *Burmese Puppets*, Oxford University Press, Singapore, 1992.

⸻, 'The Ramayana at the Burmese Court', *Arts of Asia*, November–December 1989.

Strachan, Paul, *Mandalay: Travels from the Golden City*, Kiscadale Publications, Gartmore, 1994.

Symes, Michael, *An Account of an Embassy to the Kingdom of Ava Sent by the Governor General of India in the Year 1795*, J. Debrett, Oriental Press, London, 1800.

Than Tun (ed.), *The Royal Orders of Burma, AD 1596–1885*, Pts. I–X, Center for Southeast Asian Studies, Kyoto University, Kyoto, 1983–90.

Thein Han, U and Khin Zaw, U, 'Ramayana in Burmese Literature and Arts', *Journal of the Burma Research Society*, Vol. LIX, Pts. I and II, Rangoon, December 1976.

Thiri U Zana, *In-yon-sar-tan*, Government Printing Press, Rangoon, 1962.

Tin, U, *Konbaungset Mahayazawindawgyi* [Chronicle of the Konbaung Dynasty], 3 vols., Laitimantaing Press, Rangoon, 1967.

_____, *Myanmar Min Okchokpon Sardan* [Administration under the Burmese Kings], 5 vols., Government Printing and Stationery, Rangoon, 1932–3.

Trager, Frank N. and Koenig, William J., *Burmese Sit-tans 1764–1826: Records of Rural Life and Administration*, Association for Asian Studies, University of Arizona, Tucson, 1979.

Twinthin Taik Wun Maha Sithu, *Twinthin Myanmar Yazawinthit* [Twinthin Chronicle], Mingala Press, Rangoon, 1968.

Win Maung, Maung, 'Shwe-sin-khon-pwe' [Gilded Elephant Hopping Show], *Hanthawaddy*, No. 160, Rangoon, 22 October 1972.

Over eighty Burmese language books and articles were consulted, but are too numerous to list. Moreover, the works are generally unavailable outside Burma.

Index

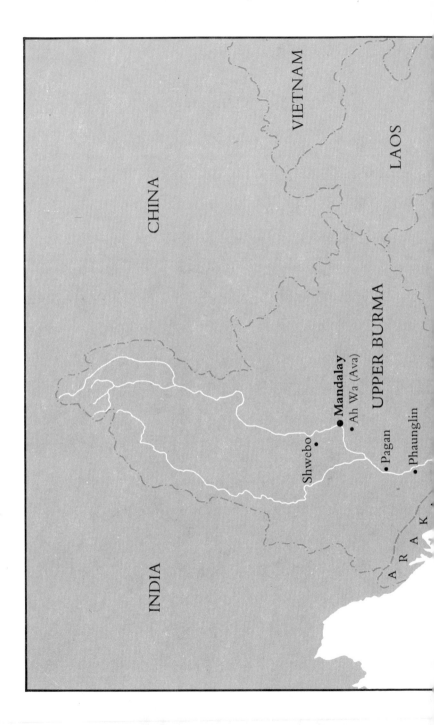